Praise for
Keep Faith Alive

"Families have been under attack since the first days of creation. Satan's strategy is well-documented throughout the Bible. Dudley has recognized that strong families are important in faith development, but a strong family with intentional grandparents is even better. When I ask my university students in class each year who shaped their faith the most, the majority list their grandparents as one of the top three influencers and spiritual guides. If you are worried about the future generation, the author has given you some practical and powerful ideas of things you can do to help your grandkids be faithful. I hope what you read on the pages of this book will inspire you and move you to make intentional grandparenting part of your family's DNA."

—**Robert Oglesby,** ACU Bible Faculty Director; ACU Center for Youth and Family Ministry

"Grandparents are our best-kept secret in faith formation! Dudley Chancey has uncovered the secret with a timely and important book—grounded in research and filled with wisdom and insight and ideas. The power of grandparents to share faith with the other generations in their family and in the congregation is still untapped. This book gives us the understanding and practical strategies to tap into that power."

—**John Roberto,** Director, Lifelong Faith Associates; author, *Lifelong Faith: Formation for All Ages and Generations*

"Chancey has given grandparents, their children, and their grandchildren an incredible resource within the pages of *Keep Faith Alive*. His research provides a treasure trove of spiritual, emotional, and practical insights that will help grandparents of all ages walk alongside their grandchildren and engage them prayerfully and conversationally in the great things God has done and is doing in our world. In addition, his counsel regarding boundaries, overall health, and our own spiritual journey as grandparents provides actionable steps for strengthening and growing our relationship with God, our children, and our grandchildren. As a grandfather of four, I encourage all grandparents who want to pass a legacy of faith to their grandchildren to pick up a copy and read *Keep Faith Alive*."

—**Dr. Gregory Anderson,** President, Midland Christian School; Assistant Director, Lipscomb University Doctorate of Ministry Program

"Using the importance of 'faith stories' as the cornerstone and weaving together research and practical application, Dudley has produced an informative and compelling book for parents and grandparents. The thesis is clear: The generations that follow will not know the stories of how God has impacted our lives unless we tell them. Rich in resources and valuable suggestions, the volume is a must-read for anyone seeking more information in transferring their legacy of faith."

—**Dr. Jerry and Lynn Jones**

"When I became a parent, I went on a search for books to read and mentors to follow. That is exactly what I had to do again following my 'birth' as a grandmother. Grandparenting, whether by blood or by spiritual connection, is a vital role in the life of a child. Not only is this role essential for the children, but it is also extremely important for grandparents. Research is clear that people don't fear their own deaths as much as they fear that their lives won't have mattered. With intentional grandparenting, we can know our time on earth matters. This book offers beautiful ways to make sure that this happens!"

—**Beverly Ross,** MA, LPC-S, Founder and Executive Director of Wise County Christian Counseling and Jenny's Hope; coauthor of *Scarred Hope: A Mother and Son Learn to Carry Grief and Live with Joy*

"Dudley Chancey has written a book that will be useful to many different readers. While maintaining a strong biblical base, the book surveys numerous academic studies and thus serves as a helpful resource for church leaders and ministers who will appreciate summaries of the findings of leading researchers. The book gives practical advice for grandparents who are seeking ways to connect with and influence grandchildren, clearly focusing on spiritual influences. Included are numerous suggested resources for grandparents. The book gives suggestions for developing one's spiritual life more fully. Finally, the book provides help and encouragement for those who desire to tell their own faith stories more effectively."

—**Bob Young,** DMin, Latin American Leadership Development

"Dudley Chancey has provided a great service to the church through his carefully researched book on grandparenting and how grandparents pass faith on to their grandchildren through storytelling. His objective was to explore 'intentional intergenerational living' where grandparents tell their grandchildren about the great things that God has done for them. This construct is defined as 'telling our faith story—telling the greatest things that God has done and is doing in our world.' This isn't just a book for grandparents; it is a book for anyone who is interested in how faith is passed from one generation to the next. It is a book for parents, youth workers, ministers, church members, and scholars. Although the book is academic in its approach to the topic, it is accessible to every reader because of its pastoral tone. Chancey shares his research, but he also shares his heart and his concern for intentional intergenerational faith. As a grandparent, I'm grateful for this book. After reading the book, I am more intentional about passing my faith story on to my grandchildren. Perhaps that is the greatest attribute of this work: It causes the reader to reflect on how to make changes in their own lives to be more intentional in their intergenerational living. It helps the reader understand the importance of telling our personal God-story to others."

—**G. Steve Kinnard,** Editor of *Teleios*, a journal of holistic Christian spirituality; Educational Director, Chord Leadership Center

"I started reading this book with a heavy heart and a sinking feeling. Distance, an overly busy schedule, and friction with our children has hindered the influence we had on our grandchildren. I know the biblical admonitions. I also know I want to do better with our eight. In the book, I expected a guilt trip. Although it is scholarly at times and heavily footnoted, what I discovered was a breath of fresh air: motivation and encouragement to pass this precious faith on to the next generation."

—**Joe Castillo,** BBS, MDiv, Artist, Author, and Storyteller

"This is one opportunity that is often overlooked and neglected. And—it may be right in front of us! The author of this book articulates a spiritual vision for grandparents that can help anyone learn how to make a lasting kingdom investment in their grandchildren. While parents are still to be the primary spiritual guides for their children, grandparents have a rich opportunity to participate in their spiritual formation and growth.

As the grandfather to four grandchildren, I read this book not just with casual interest but as a guide to help me learn how to be more intentional in sharing the story of my faith in Jesus with my own grandchildren. For me, this has been a great reminder of the powerful ministry of grandparenting."

—**Jim Martin,** Vice President, Harding School of Theology

"Christian grandparents will surely want to strengthen their spiritual influence on their precious grandchildren, and this book gives clear guidance. The author has carefully and diligently spent the last few years gathering research data by survey and interviews on effective spiritual grandparenting. Now in this unique book, the author shares his findings on what makes a strong and highly effective grandparent and how to do it.

This must-read book for grandparents is solidly based on biblical principle. Relationship with one's grandchildren forms the next layer. Next, the author stresses the importance of being intentional in sharing your own faith and other spiritual values. The author highlights the example of the psalmist in emphasizing the importance of telling children the great things that God has done and is doing around the world. He also stresses the importance of grandparents sharing their own faith with their grandchildren. Numerous statistical charts give the reader an objective look at many aspects of grandparenting for a purpose. One can evaluate their own style and see what works with kids and what does not."

—**Lynn McMillon,** PhD, Distinguished Professor of Bible, Emeritus; Licensed Marital and Family Therapist, Retired

"In years past, no one questioned the impact of grandparents on the lives of children. Even with the vast changes over the years, grandparents remain unique stewards of a lifelong faith that only they can share. There is undeniable power in a 'praying grandparent,' especially when a grandparent takes seriously the call to 'declare your power to the next generation' (Ps. 71:18). *Keep Faith Alive* not only makes a clear case for the role of grandparents, but it also provides clear, accessible, and powerful ways grandparents can engage their grandchildren that pass on the love and mission of Jesus Christ with authentic connection and compassion. This is a book to not just read but to study, dog-ear, drink in, and commit to practicing daily."

—**Chap Clark,** PhD, Author, *Hurt 2.0: Inside the World of Today's Teenagers*; Executive Director, Institute for Ministry Leadership

"Many grandparents, after parenting their own children, find themselves part of bringing up the grandchildren. Dudley Chancey calls us to make sure passing on our faith is part of this role. He not only issues that challenge, but he explores many ways for grandparents to help raise up faithful grandchildren. This book is filled with excellent practices to help us be better grandparents. We felt affirmed by this thorough study in the efforts we are making to tell our own faith stories about the great things God has done."

—**Sally and Harold Shank,** Edmond, Oklahoma

"While Chancey is credible and justified in having *opinions* about grandparenting, what made this book unique and compelling for me was the extensive *research* study that informs every page (in addition to Scripture). Since I'm not yet a grandparent, I assumed most of my thoughts while reading would be about a 'someday in the future' application for me. Instead, I was constantly reminded of my parents and in-laws and the massive, positive role they played in the lives of my (now adult) children. Thank God for intentional, loving, faith-filled grandparents!"

—**Mark Oestreicher,** Author, Founder of The Youth Cartel

"Grandparents matter . . . more than those of us who are now grandparents realize or know. Our grandkids are growing up in a world that's catechizing them 24-7, all too often in ways that are opposed to the gospel and things that are good, true, right, and honorable. And now more than ever the presence and voice of grandparents is needed in the lives of our grandkids so that they might hear and heed the call of Jesus to 'Come and follow me.' Do your grandkids a favor and read this book!"

—**Dr. Walt Mueller,** President, The Center for Parent/Youth Understanding

"All grandparents have an image of the perfect grandparent. Sometimes we struggle to become what we want to be. If you don't have the relationship with your grandchildren that you have always wanted, Chancey can help you get there. The product of fresh and extensive research about grandparenting and faith transmission, *Keep Faith Alive* will provide encouragement and inspiration for every grandparent who desires to connect with their grandchildren and build a lasting legacy with and for them. Full of practical ideas and personal anecdotes, and fully centered on spiritual principles, this is a great resource for Christian grandparents or those who are wanting to prepare for grandparenthood."

—**Teresa Castleman,** Director, Abundant Living, a ministry for Christian senior adults sponsored by Harding University

"If you're a grandparent (or plan to become one someday), this book will be a great encouragement to you. Grandparents are often marginalized in a world that values staying young, relevant, productive, and tech-savvy. But the truth is—our grandchildren need grandparents a whole lot more than they need coolness and the latest tech knowledge. Today's 'cut-flower' grandkids need roots, and that's what we can give them. I'm so glad that Dudley has written this very excellent guidebook for grandparents who want to have a lasting impact on their grandkids' lives and pass on a legacy of faith."

—**Wayne Rice,** Author, Co-host, *Legacy Grandparenting* podcast

"As I read through this timely piece by Dr. Dudley Chancey, I was reminded of the passage in the book of Judges where the writer states that 'there arose another generation after them who did not know the LORD or the work that he had done for Israel' (2:10 ESV). We are foolish to think that this would never happen again, and Dr. Chancey's encouragement of spiritual leadership from grandparents is a key ingredient to prevention. This reading should not only be read by grandparents and soon-to-be grandparents but also by those who are currently parenting their own children. Parents should use as many tools as possible to prayerfully help our children navigate this spiritually deficient world. Grandparents should be a part of that toolbox."

—**Dr. Bill Pink,** President, Ferris State University, Big Rapids, Michigan

"The decline of faith among young people in the US is well-documented and sobering. Sadly, far more ink has been spilled in recent literature on diagnosis than treatment. In *Keep Faith Alive*, Chancey takes a different approach, making the case that the greatest latent strength of faith transmission is right in front of our eyes—with grandparents. Using Scripture, social science, original research, and plenty of personal anecdotes, the author offers convincing arguments as well as concrete practices to empower grandparents to take a more prominent role in the spiritual development of their grandchildren. This will be a groundbreaking playbook for intergenerational faith formation for years to come.

—**Phil Brookman,** Lead Minister, Memorial Road Church of Christ

"For parents, it is not wise to want something for your children that you aren't willing to pursue for yourself. We want the next generation to have a compelling story of Jesus to live into, and this story must be modeled, not downloaded. With a few years of research and decades of ministry experience, Dudley writes a book encouraging each generation to take seriously how we pass along faith to the generations that come after us. In reading this book, you will be inspired and encouraged to live a life of meaning and purpose. The next generation is watching."

—**Josh Ross,** Lead Minister at Sycamore View Church in Memphis; author of a few books, most recently *COREOLOGY: Six Principles for Navigating an Election Season without Losing Our Witness*

"As we viewed a video of the first sonogram of our newest grandchild punctuated by the rapid heartbeat of a nine-week-old fetus, we were awed by LIFE and our role in it: grandparents. Dr. Chancey provides encouragement and how-to as a valuable tool for grandparents of one or twenty-one! This book combines sound research and practical applications in stand-alone chapters for grandparents of varying skills. Keep this manual close as you enjoy your journey as a GRAND parent."

—**Betty and Steve Gregg,** our co-grandparents for Crosby Kyle Chancey, born March 19, 2025

"When Paul sought to strengthen the faith and galvanize the courage of Timothy, he evoked the name of Timothy's grandmother, Lois (among other things). In this well-researched and challenging book, Chancey reminds us of the vital role grandparents can play in the lives of both their children and grandchildren. We often hear of the joys and privilege of being a grandparent—something to which I can testify—but to go hand in glove with the privilege is a deep sense of calling. We can be guides, affirmers, encouragers, and evangelists. I'm especially grateful for the suggestions of how to be intentional in passing along our stories of faith to our grandkids."

—**Mike Cope,** Director of Ministry Outreach, Pepperdine University

KEEP FAITH ALIVE

KEEP FAITH ALIVE

GRANDPARENTS AND A GODLY LEGACY

DUDLEY CHANCEY

Abilene Christian University Press

KEEP FAITH ALIVE

Grandparents and a Godly Legacy

 | ISBN 978-1-68426-222-9 | LCCN 2024057218

Printed in the United States of America

LIBRARY OF CONGRESS CATALOGING-IN-PUBLICATION DATA
Names: Chancey, Dudley, 1953- author.
Title: Keep faith alive : grandparents and a godly legacy.
Description: Abilene, Texas : ACU Press, [2025] | Includes bibliographical references.
Identifiers: LCCN 2024057218 (print) | LCCN 2024057219 (ebook) | ISBN 9781684262229 (paperback) | ISBN 9781684268450 (ebook)
Subjects: LCSH: Grandparenting—Religious aspects—Christianity. | Grandparent and child—Religious aspects—Christianity. | Spiritual formation—Churches of Christ.
Classification: LCC BV4528.5 .C42 2025 (print) | LCC BV4528.5 (ebook) | DDC 248.8/45—dc23/eng/20250328
LC record available at https://lccn.loc.gov/2024057218
LC ebook record available at https://lccn.loc.gov/2024057219

Cover design by Outerwear | Interior text design by Sandy Armstrong, Strong Design

For information contact:
Abilene Christian University Press | ACU Box 29138 | Abilene, Texas 79699
1-877-816-4455 | www.acupressbooks.com

25 26 27 28 29 30 31 // 7 6 5 4 3 2 1

This book is dedicated to Ken and Sharron Davidson.

Thank you for your desire to see young people know Christ and his church.

Contents

Foreword

I've known Dudley Chancey since long before he became a grand-parent or probably even considered writing a book on the subject. To me, Dudley is one of the most remarkable individuals I know. He is not only a friend and partner in work with youth and families but also an exceptional leader who influences those who make a difference. Dudley is a devoted husband, a loving father, and now a proud grandfather. I hold him in the highest regard and have great admiration for him. So when Dudley shared the manuscript for this book with me, I eagerly anticipated reading it, and it did not disappoint. His skill in crafting a well-researched, inspiring, yet practical book on grandparenting is evident in the pages of the book you now hold.

All around the world, our children are being bombarded with mixed messages from the culture, many of which conflict with a biblical worldview. In the United States alone, there are sixty-seven million grandparents who have the potential to profoundly shape and influence their grandchildren's lives. Those of us involved in this remarkable "God movement" known as family ministry, like Dudley, have witnessed the rise of a new wave of church and parachurch ministries dedicated to supporting grandparents. We've seen churches introduce classes and groups specifically for grandparents, and a growing number of resources are being published to support them. Personally, I could spend every week of the year speaking about topics like "Doing Life with Your Adult Children," "Finding Joy in the Empty Nest," and "Being a Grandparent May Be Your Greatest Legacy."

Grandparents are leaning into their calling in greater ways than ever before. They are becoming more intentional about their legacy role while becoming more concerned about this ever-changing culture. *Keep Faith Alive* will help grandparents and others leading grandparent ministries become more effective in their role. Research tells us that parents are the greatest spiritual influence in their children's lives, but right behind them are the grandparents. How many times have you heard someone mention that it was the loving and prayerful faith of a grandmother that helped keep them grounded in their faith? As you begin to read this book, here are three principles that may help you be the grandparent you were called to be.

Your Greatest Legacy Just May Be with Your Grandchildren

One woman said to me recently, "Now that I have grandchildren, this is my priority!" Grandparenting can be a love affair between generations. In years past, I used to hear grandparents talk with excitement about moving away from family involvement. These days, the focus has shifted more toward embracing the role of being a purposeful and loving grandparent. Honestly, that seems like a far more meaningful way to spend our time than sitting in front of the TV watching *I Love Lucy* reruns or the Golf Channel. For us personally, we're fortunate to have our grandchildren close by, and my wife even retired from teaching to be a fully involved grandmother. She now views this as her calling and a significant part of her purpose during our empty nest years. Of course, there are moments when our grandkids think we're ancient, and after a weekend of taking care of them while their parents are away, we sometimes think they might be right!

No Matter How Close or How Far You Are from Your Grandkids, You Can Be a Praying Grandparent

Make it a commitment to pray daily for your grandkids. This can be something personal and meaningful that you do that will make a difference. Tell your grandkids you are praying for them. I have made a habit for most of my adult life to keep a prayer journal. Every morning, I write out some of my prayers of adoration, confession, thanksgiving, and supplication. A few months ago, I showed my three-year-old grandson, Huxley, his name in my prayer journal, and I told him I prayed for him every day. Huxley at three can't read, and I'm sure he didn't fully understand that his "Papa J" prays for him every day. The next time I saw him, he was sitting on my lap, and he said, "Show me my name." I looked at him not fully understanding what he wanted. And then he picked up my journal and handed it to me. He would not have understood that my eyes immediately welled up with tears. Praying for your grandchildren is a tangibly eternal job for you.

Be the "Party Time" Grandparents

Whenever you have a choice between giving your grandkids socks and underwear for Christmas or a fun toy, choose the fun toy every time. Grandparents don't have to do all the heavy lifting or strong discipline; you get to choose to have serious fun. Don't underestimate the power that play and fun has on family bonding. I wish you could have met my grandma, Nene. In my world she was a “bigger than life” influence. She was a character but always the “party time grandma.” I knew when Nene came over to our house, there would be a sugary treat. She would sit down and ask me about my life and usually would suggest a fun event. I would do anything for that woman, and I knew she loved me. Be that kind of grandparent.

Yes, families can be complicated. Perhaps you’re a long-distance grandparent because your grandchildren live far away, or maybe your grandkids live under your roof. Sometimes family dynamics are challenging, with estrangement or other serious issues. Yet there’s something truly special about a dependable, loving grandmother or grandfather who can provide stability and foster well-being and healing for their grandchildren. Dudley is absolutely correct: By nurturing a God-honoring, loving relationship with your grandchildren, you can build a legacy that will endure long after you’re gone.

Jim Burns, PhD
Founder of HomeWord
Podcast: *HomeWord with Jim Burns*
Author of *Doing Life with Your Adult Children: Keep Your Mouth Shut and the Welcome Mat Out*

Acknowledgments

So, a book about grandparents. I never met my mother's parents. I think I remember seeing my dad's parents one time when I was five. My parents never got to see my children. But my two sons had the best grandmother ever: my wife Vicki's mom, Bernice. She loved them, fed them, shot .22 rifles with them, picked up pecans with them, and most importantly modeled and talked Jesus to them.

I am most grateful for my sons, Drew and Matt. They married Proverbs 31 women—Jules and Sarah. We have watched Drew and Jules telling their faith stories to our four granddaughters. Matt and Sarah welcomed their first child in March 2025. I am confident that this child will know the great things that God has done and is doing in our world.

I am most, most grateful for Vicki. She is the best grandmother ever to our grandchildren. I admire her patience and love for these and other children. I love to sit with her and the grandchildren and pray, read, and talk about the great things that God has done and is doing in our world.

I am thankful for Abilene Christian University Press (one of my alma maters) and Jason Fikes and his colleagues (Laura, Duane, Olivia, Mary, and Caitlyn) for giving me the opportunity to get this project done.

I am thankful for Sarah Bailey, Teresa Castleman, and Dr. Greg Anderson for reading and giving input on the manuscript. Your thoughts and edits made this a better project.

I am thankful for Sue Rubio who watered the seeds of this project, and for her love for her grandchildren.

I am thankful for Dr. Ron Bruner and his contribution of the chapter on grandmothers. Also, for his support and encouragement to get this done.

Each time I begin a research project I am reminded of how grateful I am to Dr. Greer Litton Fox at the University of Tennessee, Knoxville. Thank you for teaching me and for your continued friendship.

I am very thankful for the many grandparents who took the online survey and took the time to Zoom with me online. Your answers and feedback are the backbone of this project.

Thanks to the Intergenerational Faith Center and Stephen Eck. Thank you for believing that this project was important and worth all the work.

Thank you, Winterfest and NCYM, for keeping me young and motivated to share my faith story and the great things that God has done and is doing in our world to reach young people.

Introduction

Solomon said it best, "There is nothing new under the sun." He also said, "The writing of books is endless" (Eccl. 1:9; 12:12 LEB). There isn't much new in this book. It is mixed with old studies of grandparents and our recent study of grandparents. It is interwoven with old voices and young voices speaking about faith.

This Grandparent Project came about for several reasons. I am a grandparent, and I want our children and grandchildren to be Christ-followers all their lives. A second reason came from studying the book of Hosea and Psalms 71, 78, and 145. I continue to try to comprehend why people who saw firsthand the great things God was doing still walked away and turned their backs on him. Someone was not telling the next generation. Several questions arose as I laid the groundwork. Will we lose a generation of children because we failed to tell our faith story and the great things God has done and is doing in our world? What more can we learn about grandparenting specifically as it relates to the spiritual lives of our grandchildren? What can we learn from our past? What can we grasp and understand about the present? How do you envision the future for your grandchildren? Will it be with or without God?

There is Good News! With Jesus there is always Good News. The Grandparent Project results will provide ideas and encouragement to help all of us be faithful in what God has called us to do.

There is an old adage that says, "People don't care how much you know until they know how much you care." Another driving force behind this work is that I care about grandparents. I am a grandparent! Grandparenting is a big deal. In the United States approximately sixty-seven million adults are grandparents, with an average grandparent age of sixty-seven years old. While a quarter of midlife adults (forty to sixty-four) are grandparents, about 70 percent of adults sixty-five and older are grandparents. Grandparents matter! There is an increasing number of grandparents raising grandchildren in our country due to divorce, drug abuse, and single moms having to work several jobs. The good news for these grandparents is that some churches and local and state agencies are providing educational, financial, and emotional support to address many concerns of grandparents today.

Perhaps the largest driving force behind this work is our desire to help grandparents share their faith story and the great things God has done and is doing in our world—with their grandchildren. When the apostle John writes in 3 John 1:4, "I have no greater joy than to hear that my children are walking in the truth," I can relate. Vicki and I have done many great things in this world, but nothing tops sitting with our grandchildren and hearing them pray and discuss Bible stories. I pray this for all of you reading this book, that you will have opportunities to share your faith story with your grandchildren.

The Grandparent Project grew out of several Zoom sessions that I did with grandparent friends and acquaintances around the country. From the information I gathered, I put together an online survey. I sent the survey link out to churches all over the United States. I also gave the link to churches where I presented the initial background information and the topics I was pursuing about how grandparents do or do not share their faith story with their grandchildren. I ended up with 995 completed surveys. The online survey collected demographic data as well as data about grandparents' church attendance, health, faith practices with grandchildren, legacy, styles and roles, raising grandchildren, supports, and what successful grandparents do in sharing their faith.

The sample participants from the survey were well-educated. Financially, only 1 percent of the sample was below the poverty level. Most of the participants were sixty-five to seventy-five years old. Sixty-seven percent of the sample participants were female, which is typical in social science research projects. Ninety-five percent were Caucasian. Eighty percent of the sample participants were married. Seventy-four percent vote Republican. Fifty-six percent of the sample was retired, with 31 percent still working full-time. The church affiliation consisted of over eight hundred members of Churches of Christ, with the remaining sample consisting of Disciples of Christ, Independent Christian, Baptist, Methodist, Church of God, Catholic, Lutheran, Presbyterian, Anglican, and several from nondenominational Bible churches.

Combining the online surveys, interviews, and teaching trips, I offer the following Grandparent Project results and comments with reflection and discussion questions at the end of each chapter for a deeper dive into this important topic of faith.

Whether you are reading this book alone, with your spouse, with your children, or in a small group, my prayer is that you will be encouraged. Encouraged to tell your faith story and the great things that God has done and is doing in your life, with your grandchildren, and with the children in your church.

Dudley (2025)

CHAPTER ONE

Grandparenting

Past, Present, and Future

Marley was dead, to begin with. . . . Old Marley was as dead as a door-nail.

—Charles Dickens, *A Christmas Carol*

When I think of the past, the present, and the future, I think of *A Christmas Carol.* Charles Dickens does a masterful job of getting Ebenezer Scrooge to reflect on his life—past, present, and future. Dickens uses the ghost of Marley to confront Scrooge and eventually get him to change his life—to turn his life around.

One of the driving forces behind this grandparent study was a study I did of Israel and Judah in the Old Testament, specifically the up-and-down relationship they had with God. God's chosen people would forget where they came from (the Exodus) and what they were given (the Promised Land). God used men and women (prophets and judges) to plead with the people to return to him. I believe a strong case can be made that Israel was not carrying out the commands of Deuteronomy 6 or Psalm 71, 78, and 145. They were not telling the next generation about the great things God had done for them. They were not telling the next generation where their prosperity had come from. They were not telling their faith story.

The Old Testament book of Hosea may be a very prophetic book for us today. Hosea spent forty years trying to get the Northern Kingdom (Israel) to repent, to come back to Jehovah God. He preached about their past, the present, and what would happen in the future. They failed to tell their children the great things God had done. When times got bad, they were so out of touch with their heritage that they called on the Baal gods for help. They never turned back to God.

In 722 BC, Assyria comes in and conquers the Northern Kingdom. They kill some, sell some, and take the rest away captive. We never hear of the northern ten tribes again—ever. Judah down south is not far from some of the same treatment. In 586 BC Babylon conquers Jerusalem, destroys Solomon's temple and the city, and takes most of the people away as captives to Babylon. When one looks at Israel's past, present, and future in the Bible, you would think that we today would be like Ebenezer Scrooge and mend our ways.

While thinking about Israel's and Judah's response to God, I considered how I might be responding as a Christ-follower, especially in my new role as a grandparent. What does the past, present, and future look like for grandparenting? The purpose of this book is to (1) look at how grandparents have (or have not) told their children and grandchildren their faith story and the great things God has done and is doing in our world, (2) show how grandparents are doing (or not doing) today from our research, and (3) share ideas and suggestions on how we proceed in the future to make sure we are telling the next generations our faith story and the great things our God has done and is doing in our world.

Introduction—A Little Background

To begin, perhaps one of the most important kingdom ideas presented in this work is that of *intentional intergenerational living.*[1] Telling our children and grandchildren about the great things God has done that we read about in Deuteronomy 6, in Psalm 71, 78, and 145, and in Matthew 28 and Mark 16 should teach us that this is more than a parent thing. It is more than a grandparent thing. It is a community and church responsibility. We all have a major role in telling our children and grandchildren our faith story and the great things God has done and is doing in our world. Reflect for a moment on the passage below from Psalm 78:1–7.

> My people, hear my teaching; listen to the words of my mouth. I will open my mouth with a parable; I will utter hidden things, things from of old—things we have heard and known, things our ancestors have told us. We will not hide them from their descendants; we will tell the next generation the praiseworthy deeds of the LORD, his power, and the wonders he has done. He decreed statutes for Jacob and established the law in Israel, which he commanded our ancestors to teach their children, so the next generation would know them, even the children yet to be born, and they in turn would tell their children. Then they would put their trust in God and would not forget his deeds but would keep his commands.

[1] I define "intentional intergenerational living" as the intentional act of involving three or more generations together purposefully to share life-on-life. This is different than being in a room with different generations present but not interacting between the generations (like most Sunday morning church services). This would be multigenerational. There is a big difference.

In the New Testament, the apostle Paul reminds readers of how young Timothy grew in his faith, the fruit of three generations of intentional intergenerational telling of the story. There are other biblical references that speak to the importance of the next generation knowing and obeying God for the good of the children (and to their detriment for not knowing and obeying God). Jewish writings speak of the spiritual aspects of parenting, with the parent seen as the representative of God. As representative, it is the parents' task to teach their children Torah. The parent who does this is the real parent—even if not biological.

To prepare for the Grandparent Project, I researched different religious groups to see if there were any patterns in the ways that they told the story of their faith. The faith traditions I explored vary in the way they teach and raise up the next generation of believers. In 2022 I was having a Bible study and meal at our house with a Muslim student attending one of my Bible classes at university. He lives in a four-generation household. They pray together every day as a family. They read from the Qur'an every day as a family. He explained the daily prayers and readings were done so that they would continue to tell their faith story about Mohammed and Allah. His grandfather told them daily that if there was no teaching and telling their faith story, it would lead them to be a part of an evil generation.

Evangelicals average about 60 percent retention, while mainline Protestants are holding around 30 percent. Other religious fellowships have much higher retention of their young people than Protestants and Catholics (Amish and Mormons). A report on a specific Protestant group showed almost a 50 percent loss of members by 2050.[2] The report was of interest to us because of the following factors listed that affect the 50 percent decline: (1) the graying of members, (2) the loss of younger generational groups, (3) a lack of effective evangelism, and (4) a failure to plant churches. The first two of these will resonate in the pages of this book.

With so many turning from faith in God, it is normal for us to wonder whether our faith will have any children.[3] Are so many walking away from church because it is boring and not relevant, or is it because the older generations did not stress the importance of a strong faith that believes in the great things that God has done and is doing in our world? While I believe it could be some of both, I strongly believe we have dropped the ball in the act of telling the story of our faith to the next generations.

I am a grandparent. I adore my grandchildren. I want our grandchildren to know Jesus Christ and have a relationship with him and his church all their lives. This fact is another driving force behind the Grandparent Project. It specifically explores how grandparents can help shape and tell their faith story to their grandchildren directly, and how grandparents can assist their children so that they can tell their children their own faith story. The main outcome of the Grandparent Project is to provide insight into how grandparents, parents, and churches can help young people spiritually mature in a way that would endear Jesus and his church to them.

---

[2]Tim Woodroof and Stan Granberg, "The Status of Churches of Christ," presentation of research project with 100 Churches of Christ, presented at Oklahoma Christian University, September 2019. Access a PDF version, "Churches of Christ in 2050," at https://www.interimministrypartners.com/report/.

[3]Dr. John Westerhoff famously asked this question in the revised edition of *Will Our Children Have Faith?* (Morehouse Publishing, 2000).

Faith Transmission—Passing on Faith—Handing Down Faith

Defining terms and concepts is very important. It is critical that everyone be on the same page as far as knowing what is being discussed. We may say, "I want to be found faithful," or "I want my children to be faithful." What is it that we mean?

"Faith" as a religious construct is difficult to define and even more difficult to quantify and measure. In chapter 11 of the book of Hebrews, we find, "Now faith is confidence in what we hope for and assurance about what we do not see" (11:1 NIV). A few pages over in chapter two of the book of James, the author has a discussion of faith and works. He makes the claim that faith without works is dead. He says he can show his faith by what he does (his works). So it seems that faith itself cannot be seen, but we can see results of someone who has faith.

Another challenge I have come across is the phrase "the faith." Several exclusive religious bodies claim that they have "the faith." No other religious body has "the faith—the truth" but them. All other religions are missing the boat. Even within certain Protestant religious bodies there is dissention about which part of the fellowship really has "the faith." Others define "the faith" as being faithful to their particular church. Participants in the Grandparent Project would say, "I want him to be a good Baptist." "It would kill me if he does not remain a good Catholic." "It is the most important thing in the world to me that my children remain faithful to the Church of Christ."

For those of you who may have taken the Grandparent Project survey, you will recall that the original title of the survey had to do with faith and values transmission. The deeper I got into focus group interviews with grandparents and studying the results of the Internet survey, the more I realized that there was no real consensus on the construct that I wanted to convey about faith for our grandchildren. The most-used construct in social science research is "faith transmission" or "transmission of faith." Recent titles of books from research include the concepts of "passing on the faith" and "handing down the faith."

A definition of "faith transmission" remains elusive. The authors of *Families and Faith* define "transmission" as "long-term efforts by parents to teach something they feel is highly desirable to their child, such as religious values, beliefs, and practices."[4] In the pursuit of a working definition of faith transmission for the Grandparent Project, several other questions and thoughts began to surface. For example:

- What exactly is *the* faith?
- Do we confuse "faith" and "spirituality" with "religion" and "religious traditions"?
- Is people's faith or *the* faith what Scripture has mandated us to pass on?
- Is this "passing on" a one-time thing, or is it continual?

As I searched for the idea that I wanted to convey in this study, I became well-informed about other behaviors that families transmit across generations (e.g., relationship/partner violence, risk, attachment, abuse and trauma, parenting behavior, substance abuse, personality structure). In these examples, the transmission takes place between three or more generations. This is good news, in a sense, to know that we can transmit behaviors, which means we can transmit our faith to the next generations as we have been asked to do in Scripture. So what exactly do we want our children and grandchildren to have, to know, to give to their children and grandchildren? I grew up in very conservative Churches of Christ in Georgia. We were taught that being faithful consisted

[4]Vern L. Bengtson, *Families and Faith: How Religion Is Passed Down across Generations* (Oxford University Press, 2013).

of attending the Church of Christ at least three times a week and giving money in the offering as you had been prospered that week. We had lesson books that we took home and filled out for the next meeting. We had to do our Bible lessons before we did our school homework. I remember getting baptized in one of those churches. You got a star and asterisk by your name to indicate that you were a faithful member of that church. That meant a lot to me as a child. Being faithful for me today includes attending church and giving, but it is so much more than that. I want my grandchildren to know the "so much more" about Jesus.

Telling Our Faith Story

You will have noticed that I chose to use the construct of "telling our faith story—telling the great things God has done and is doing in our world" to write this book about the Grandparent Project. "One generation commends your works to another; they *tell* of your mighty acts" (Ps. 145:4—emphasis mine). It is the story of God that we are to pass on! So many churches and even our participants in this study are more concerned with "getting it right about their faith tradition" than telling the great things God has done and is doing in our world. Getting women's roles, music, terminology, politics, and the color of the carpet right were more important than telling their faith story to their children and grandchildren. More about this in the coming chapters.

While I am committed to good academic rigor in research, for the Grandparent Project I am also seeking guidance from Scripture for answers and patterns of behavior that may give insight as to the rise and fall of the generations. The answers will come from social science and theology. The Bible tells the amazing story of God's chosen people—not just Israel, but all of us.[5] It is

---

[5] 1 Peter 2:9–10.

apparent that someone told Joshua of the good works of God. In his farewell speech at the end of the book of Joshua, he challenges the people of Israel to obey and keep the covenant that God has made with them. And they do—for that generation.

Some of the saddest words in Scripture, in reference to telling the great things God has done and is doing in the world, follow closely behind the end of the book of Joshua. The book of Judges begins the repeated cycle of Israel knowing God and then not knowing God. "After that whole generation had been gathered to their ancestors, another generation grew up who knew neither the LORD nor what he had done for Israel" (Judg. 2:10). How is "the telling about God" lost in one generation?

Why "Telling the Story" Has Faded in Our Time

Religion in general has been marginalized in most scientific communities and most college campuses until recently. Researchers have attempted to connect faith to measurable human values and show that it can be useful in studying individuals and families.[6] Robert Wuthnow makes several arguments that point to a decline in the church's influence and a rise in people having "faith" in science, technology, the atomic bomb, going to the moon, and all of the new toys and gadgets that everyone had to have. In 1958 surveys begin to show a dramatic drop in church attendance. What does this have to do with telling the story, telling about the great things God has done and is doing in our world, and grandparents?

Currently, churches have blamed everything from the economy, technology, and the recent COVID-19 pandemic of 2020–2021 for the drop in church attendance (which many believe is a measure of faith). Churches that shut down during COVID-19

---

[6]Diane Winston, "From Side Show to Center Stage: Mainstreaming the Study of Religion at Major Research Universities," paper presented at Annual Meetings of the American Academy of Religion, November 22, 2003.

and went online have typically not seen 100 percent of their flocks returning.[7] While churchgoers in the United States participated in person or virtually, the in-person attendance is lower than it was before COVID-19.[8] It crossed my mind that the participants in the early part of our grandparent study could have been affected by COVID-19. Could a pandemic affect one's faith? Would participants have more or less faith because of the pandemic? Similar studies in times of distress have been carried out addressing such outcomes.[9]

Grandparents in the Social Science Literature

Shifts in demographics have placed grandparents in a pivotal position. Longer lifespans, working mothers, divorce, and single-parent homes are a few of the factors that are contributing to increased involvement of grandparents in the lives of their grandchildren. I found this to be true with our participants. Research conducted in the 1930s and 1940s on grandparenting was negative.[10] This discussion changed in the 1970s with systematic research on grandparenting, generally showing grandparents in a positive light. The research shows as does this Grandparent

---

[7] Wesley J. Wildman, Joseph Bulbulia, Richard Sosis, and Uffe Schjoedt, "Religion and the COVID-19 Pandemic," *Religion, Brain & Behavior* 10, no. 2 (2020): 115–17. https://doi.org/10.1080/2153599X.2020.1749339.

[8] Pew Research Center, "How the Pandemic Has Affected Attendance at U.S. Religious Services," March 28, 2023, https://www.pewresearch.org/religion/2023/03/28/how-the-pandemic-has-affected-attendance-at-u-s-religious-services/.

[9] Greer Litton Fox and Dudley Chancey, "Sources of Economic Distress: Individual and Family Outcomes," *Journal of Family Issues* 19, no. 6 (1998): 725–49. See also Dudley Chancey, "Economic Distress and Psychological Outcomes: Using Objective and Subjective Measures of Economic Distress as Predictors of Depressive Mood and Self-Satisfaction Moderated by Religiosity" (PhD diss., University of Tennessee, 1997).

[10] For grandparenting as a negative resource, see the following: Hermann Vollmer, "The Grandmother: A Problem in Child-Rearing," *The American Journal of Orthopsychiatry* 7, no. 3 (1937): 378–82. Clifford A. Strauss, "Grandma Made Johnny Delinquent," *The American Journal of Orthopsychiatry* 13, no. 2 (1943): 343–46.

Project that more grandparents are involved with their grandchildren than in the past. It would seem with more involvement that there would be more opportunity to tell our faith story and the great things God has done and is doing in our world. This does not appear to be happening when one looks at the current state of religious participation. But is that the fault of grandparents? With this study, I believe it can be shown that this is a "yes" and "no" answer.

I believe strongly in "intentional intergenerational" relationships.[11] A family's religiosity has a positive influence on intergenerational relationships in the present and in later years. There are additional factors that are important in providing a consistent, intentional, intergenerational telling of our faith story and the great things God has done and is doing in our world. Parent and child religiosity is closely linked well into adulthood,[12] as well as other attitudes of parents that significantly predict adult children's attitudes.[13]

At least one study showed that grandparents who are tied to a community of faith (a church) are more involved with their grandchildren.[14] This tie is important, as the number one factor that prohibits many grandparent-grandchild relationships is geographical distance (this is not to be confused with "distant" grandparents). I found this distance factor to be important in this study.

---

[11] Ron Bruner and Dudley Chancey, "Why You Should Be Teaching an Intergenerational Ministry Course in Your Youth Ministry Curriculum," peer-reviewed paper presented at Association of Youth Ministry Educators Conference, 2013.

[12] Scott M. Myers, "An Interactive Model of Religiosity Inheritance: The Importance of Family Context," *American Sociological Review* 61 (1996): 858–66.

[13] Terry L. Mills and Janet M. Wilmoth, "Intergenerational Differences and Similarities in Life-Sustaining Treatment Attitudes and Decision Factors," *Family Relations* 51, no. 1 (2002): 46–54.

[14] Valarie King and Glen H. Elder Jr., "Are Religious Grandparents More Involved Grandparents?," *Journal of Gerontology* 54B, no. 6 (1999): S317–S328.

When researchers single out male and female participants, they report that mothers tend to be more religious than fathers, asserting that mothers are the primary transmitters of religious faith and practices in the family.[15] In this grandparent study, I wanted to make sure that fathers and grandfathers were highlighted as much as the data would allow. Grandfathers can play an important role in parenting and grandparenting. The 1970s, 1980s, and 1990s affirm the significance of fathers' influence on their children's faith and religious practices.[16] This study also confirms the positive influence that grandfathers can play in the lives of their children and grandchildren.

How Do Grandparents Tell the Story and the Great Things God Has Done?

Hopefully this Grandparent Project will shed some light on how this is being done (or not) today. Since embarking on this study, I have bought many grandparenting books and articles about grandparents.

There are studies reporting that a key function of grandparenthood involves transmitting faith (its origins, memory, and values) to grandchildren.[17] I want to be very clear that I believe parents are the main influencers (for good or bad) in the lives of their children. While this is critical, the Shema in Deuteronomy 6:4–9 also includes the faith community and reminds us that "it takes

---

[15] Barna Research, "Christian Women Today, Part 1 of 4: What Women Think of Faith, Leadership and Their Role in the Church," Barna, August 13, 2012, https://www.barna.com/research/christian-women-today-part-1-of-4-what-women-think-of-faith-leadership-and-their-role-in-the-church/.

[16] Lori Baker-Sperry, "Passing On the Faith: The Father's Role in Religious Transmission," *Sociological Focus* 34, no. 3 (2001): 185–98.

[17] Donald B. Conroy and Charles J. Fahey, "Christian Perspective on the Role of Grandparents," in *Grandparenthood*, ed. Vern L. Bengtson and Joan Robertson (Sage Publishing, 1985), 195–207.

a village."[18] It takes a village and a community of adults of faith that parents intentionally connect with their children to assist them as they go through the different stages of their spiritual development.[19]

Although many grandparents have a choice to tell their faith story and the great things God has done and is doing in our world, there are some cases where grandparents are not allowed to tell, or even have access to, their grandchildren. Some parents choose to be "gatekeepers" between grandparents and grandchildren.[20] I found this "gatekeeper" construct to be present in my survey and in several anecdotal interviews in this grandparent study. Noted in a 2009 study is the fact that even when grandparents positively influence their grandchildren's religious values, the impact of these values has been declining, even when those faith values are considered the most important by grandparents.[21]

In anecdotal interviews with adult (over age eighteen) grandchildren preparing for this Grandparent Project, I did not hear of any grandparents who intentionally told their faith story or the great things God has done and is doing in their world. This

---

[18] Hillary R. Clinton, *It Takes a Village* (Simon and Schuster, 1996). See also Soleman Baun and Nini Adelina Tanamal, "The Concept of 'Shema' in Deuteronomy 6:4–5 as an Application of Educational Theology," *KnE Social Sciences* 9, no. 22 (2024): 458–66, https://doi.org/10.18502/kss.v9i22.16852.

[19] Christian Smith, Bridget Ritz, and Michael Rotolo, *Religious Parenting: Transmitting Faith and Values in Contemporary America* (Princeton University Press, 2020). See also Christian Smith and Amy Adamczyk, *Handing Down the Faith* (Oxford University Press, 2021).

[20] William Austin, Marsha K. Pruitt, H. D. Kirkpatrick, James R. Flens, and Jonathan W. Gould, "Parental Gatekeeping and Child Custody/Child Access Evaluation: Part 1: Conceptual Framework, Research, and Application," *Family Court Review* 51, no. 3 (2013): 485–501. Madonna H. Meyer and Amra Kandic, "Grandparenting in the United States," *Innovation in Aging* 1, no. 2 (2017).

[21] Vern L. Bengtson, Casey E. Copen, Norella M. Putney, and Merril Silverstein, "A Longitudinal Study of the Intergenerational Transmission of Religion," *International Sociology* 24 (2009): 325–45. See also Casey E. Copen and Merril Silverstein, "Transmission of Religious Beliefs across Generations: Do Grandparents Matter?" *Journal of Comparative Family Studies* 38 (2007): 497–510.

grandparent study looked at direct and indirect ways that grandparents were involved spiritually in the lives of their grandchildren (i.e., directly by praying with them, reading the Bible with them, telling them their faith story, taking them on a mission trip; or indirectly by example, telling them they are praying for them). Some of the interviewees mentioned being taken to church when they visited grandparents. I believe that intentional, direct methods of telling their faith story and the great things God has done and is doing in their lives will be more effective than indirect methods.

What We Know and Why Grandparents Matter

Parents are—bottom line—the greatest influence on their children. This is good news and bad news. If you are a grandparent reading this, you may be wondering whether you parented well enough in telling your faith story or the great things God has done and is doing in your life to your child—the parent of your grandchildren—who in turn should be telling their faith story or the great things God has done and is doing in their lives to your grandchildren. Remember, parents are the greatest influence on their children, *not you as the grandparent*. Take heart, though. You can and do have influence on your grandchildren if you have access to them. You can and should tell your faith story and the great things God has done and is doing in your life with your grandchildren. Fifty-four published studies reveal the following:

- Foundations for faith are laid in childhood.
- The role and responsibility of the family is central in telling your faith story and the great things God has done and is doing in your life (a theological assertion as well as an observation of child development theory).
- Enduring adolescent and adult believers are largely the product of caring, supportive, stable homes where faith is seen, heard, and experienced.

- Modeling is key: Parents need to "be" and "do" what they want their child to become.[22]

The 2005 landmark National Study on Youth and Religion about churched adolescents found that teenagers will be just a little less religious than their parents.[23] This is good news if you are a parent leading a very consistent, faithful life in your walk with God. Parenting styles (authoritarian, authoritative, permissive, and uninvolved) predict children's continued practice of faith from their parents. The construct of warmth is also a predictor of parents who are successful in telling their faith story and the great things God has done and is doing in their lives.[24] Quality of relationships in the home and better marriages between husbands and wives provide more successful times for parents to tell their faith story and the great things God has done and is doing in our world.

Grandparents can be a major part of the four results mentioned in the previous list. They can lay foundations, they can provide a family atmosphere for their children and grandchildren, they can be supportive to the parents, and they can model their faith. Just as important, grandparents can speak to the importance of telling your own faith story and the great things God has done and is doing in your life in their churches and to other families. Young parents and parents-to-be need to hear that this telling starts in the womb.

---

[22]Olwyn Mark, *Passing On Faith* (Theos, 2016).

[23]Christian Smith and Melina L. Denton, *Soul Searching: The Religious and Spiritual Lives of American Teenagers* (Oxford University Press, 2005).

[24]David C. Dollahite, Loren D. Marks, Kate P. Babcock, Betsy H. Barrow, and Andrew H. Rose, "Beyond Religious Rigidities: Religious Firmness and Religious Flexibility as Complementary Loyalties in Faith Transmission," *Religions* 10 (2019). Thomas J. Schofield, Rand D. Conger, and Tricia K. Neppl, "Positive Parenting, Beliefs about Parental Efficacy, and Active Coping: Three Sources of Intergenerational Resilience," *Journal of Family Psychology* 6 (2014): 973–78. Miriam K. Ehrensaft, Heather M. Knous-Westfall, and Patricia Cohen, "Direct and Indirect Transmission of Relationship Functioning across Generations," *Journal of Family Psychology* 25 (2011): 942–52.

The intergenerational messages that grandparents can provide our churches are invaluable. The research shows that quality of relationships, unity of traditions, and stability of the family structure are keys to having opportunities to share with your grandchildren. Grandparents who have "kept the faith" need to share their stories with their children and grandchildren as well as other young people in their churches and communities. As children get older and begin to differentiate from their parents, grandparents can be there as another voice affirming the continued faith formation that began with the parents. Adolescents learn from modeling. Seeing their parents and grandparents "practice what they preach" is a very powerful way to learn their faith story and the great things God has done and is doing in their life.[25]

Moving Forward

So how did the participants in this grandparent study do? Will we lose another generation of children because we failed to tell our faith story and the great things God has done and is doing in our lives? What more can we learn about grandparenting specifically as it relates to the spiritual lives of our grandchildren? Who are the Marleys in our lives? What can we learn from our past? What can we grasp and understand about the present? How do you envision the future for your grandchildren—with or without God? There is Good News! With Jesus there is always Good News. The results of this grandparent study will provide ideas and encouragement to help all of us be faithful in what God has called us to do.

[25] Kelly D. Schwartz, "Transformations in Parent and Friend Faith Support Predicting Adolescents' Religious Faith," *International Journal for the Psychology of Religion* 16, no. 4 (2006): 311–32.

Reflect and Discuss

1. As you think about your own church involvement history, how have you seen the church grow, and how have you seen it decline? What are some reasons for both?
2. As you look at your own generations of family, how satisfied are you with their spiritual growth?
3. What have been the greatest influences in your family's spiritual growth?
4. In your opinion, what is most needed to help families grow spiritually today?
5. Talk about thoughts you had when you first became a grandparent. When did you begin to think about how your grandchild would turn out spiritually? What made you have those thoughts? Did those initial thoughts help you to be intentional about the spiritual growth of your grandchildren?
6. They say you can't give what you don't have. Did you find yourself becoming a better person or a better student of the Bible when you became a grandparent?
7. Have you taken a grandparenting class?
8. Have you attended a conference for grandparents?
9. How could your church be more helpful in equipping grandparents to share their faith story and the great things God has done and is doing in our world?

CHAPTER TWO

The Influence of Parents

How Grandparents Can Assist

Much research has been done about children and parents. The results are always the same—parents are the number one influence in children's lives. There are hundreds of scientific articles about parental influence in every area of children's lives (e.g., education, sports, leadership, behavior, keeping/breaking rules, religion, language learning, development, worldviews). We know that we as grandparents can be influential also.

Specifically, in this short chapter, the concern is about the influence parents have on their children's religiosity and how grandparents can come along beside the parents and reinforce their children's influence on their grandchildren. Christian Smith, Bridget Ritz, and Michael Rotolo define the task of parenting as follows:

> The central joy of parents is to prepare and equip their children not only to enjoy all that is good in life but also to successfully navigate, endure, and overcome difficulties in

> their personal life journeys in the world. Good parents provision their children with the ground, learning, and resources they will need to surmount life's difficulties and come out stronger and truer on the other side. How parents do this will be shaped a lot by their own experience growing up in their families. Parents may simply enjoy their offspring as children, but the true quality of their parenting work will be tested when their children face life's trials and tribulations down the road. The demanding task of parenting is made especially difficult by two major complications: parents must never violate their children's ultimate self-determination nor trigger teenage rebellion. These demand that parents carefully navigate the narrow, difficult straights between lax and overbearing parenting.[1]

Parenting is not an easy task. There are books on prenatal care and postnatal care. Books on developing teenagers in your house. Type "raising children" into the Amazon search bar, and you get fifty thousand choices. Everyone is an expert—except the parents with the colicky baby at 3 a.m., or the parents of a teenager who isn't home at 3 a.m. Vicki and I are very appreciative of the community of people in our churches that surrounded us and our boys as we did the parent attempt.

We have been richly blessed as we watch our adult children do the parenting of our grandchildren. Many of the good things we did as parents we can see our children repeating. We are trying to come along beside and behind as we witness our grandchildren being discipled by their parents. We do want to say that there are good books to read about parenting. For example, in the book *Along the Way*, the editors combined different perspectives about

---

[1]Christian Smith, Bridget Ritz, and Michael Rotolo, *Religious Parenting: Transmitting Faith and Values in Contemporary America* (Princeton University Press, 2020), 118.

children and faith. One of the editors tells the story of redecorating his granddaughter Lily's room. Ron's wife Ann had placed stars that glow at night on the ceiling of the bedroom. A few weeks later at bedtime prayers and Bible reading, the story was from Genesis about the Creation. Lily told her mom that night that her Nina (Ann) put the stars in the sky. Ron says this about that moment:

> Those stars [on the ceiling] imitate the Creator's work and remind Lily of our larger universe. Lily is connecting her memories and story with the larger story of God; at the same time, she reminds us that we participate in the ongoing creative work of God ourselves. That's good theology. Children like Lily come to a healthy understanding of God and their spirituality when they are immersed in environments where every generation is constantly and intentionally attentive to the spiritual. Spiritual parents, and spiritual grandparents, form spiritual children and are shaped spiritually by those children.[2]

This is a good example of three generations working together to tell their faith story and the great things that God has done and is doing in our world. The influence of the parents and grandparents can be seen in the simple task of redecorating a room.

Proverbs 22:6 may be the most famous Bible verse about parenting: "Train up a child in the way he should go: and when he is old, he will not depart from it" (KJV). While there are hundreds of references in the Bible about children, fathers, and mothers, there is not a specific list of job duties for a father and mother raising children. In fact, most of the stories in the Bible concerning families are about messed-up families. Some of our favorite characters in the Bible were part of a very complicated family system, much

---

[2] Ron Bruner and Dana Kennamer Pemberton, *Along the Way: Conversations about Children and Faith* (Abilene Christian University Press, 2015), 48.

like many of our families today. Below is a list of some of the Scripture that has supplied instruction for Christian parents along the way to share their faith story and tell about the great things God has done and is doing in our world:

- "Children are a heritage from the LORD, offspring a reward from him" (Ps. 127:3).
- "Fathers, do not exasperate your children; instead, bring them up in the training and instruction of the Lord" (Eph. 6:4).
- "These commandments that I give you today are to be on your hearts. Impress them on your children" (Deut. 6:6–7).
- "We will tell the next generation the praiseworthy deeds of the LORD, his power, and the wonders he has done" (Ps. 78:4).
- "Children's children are a crown to the aged, and parents are the pride of their children" (Prov. 17:6).
- "In everything set them an example by doing what is good" (Titus 2:7).
- "Anyone who does not provide for their relatives, and especially for their own household, has denied the faith and is worse than an unbeliever" (1 Tim. 5:8).
- "Discipline your children, and they will give you peace; they will bring you the delights you desire" (Prov. 29:17).
- "Children should not have to save up for their parents, but parents for their children" (2 Cor. 12:14).
- "Honor your father and your mother, as the LORD your God has commanded you" (Deut. 5:16).
- "I have no greater joy than to hear that my children are walking in the truth" (3 John 1:4).

- "Only be careful, and watch yourselves closely so that you do not forget the things your eyes have seen or let them fade from your heart as long as you live. Teach them to your children and to their children after them" (Deut. 4:9).

Grandparents of the Grandparent Project Participants

We asked the grandparent participants to rate any spiritual influence that any or all of their grandparents had on them. Figure 2.1 below shows results:

Your Mother's Mother		Your Mother's Father	
Negative Influence	1%	Negative Influence	4%
No Influence	25%	No Influence	37%
Some Influence	26%	Some Influence	23%
Much Influence	23%	Much Influence	16%
The Most Influential	14%	The Most Influential	7%
Your Father's Mother		**Your Father's Father**	
Negative Influence	3%	Negative Influence	4%
No Influence	30%	No Influence	43%
Some Influence	27%	Some Influence	22%
Much Influence	18%	Much Influence	13%
The Most Influential	9%	The Most Influential	3%

Figure 2.1

Research shows that grandparents' involvement with their grandchildren is significantly influenced by having known their own grandparents and their history.[3] We know that many of us parented

[3]Valarie King and Glen H. Elder Jr., "The Legacy of Grandparenting: Childhood Experiences with Grandparents and Current Involvement with Grandchildren," *Journal of Marriage and the Family* 59, no. 4 (1997): 848.

much like we were parented. Even when we said, "I will never do that to my kid," we often did the same thing. There is some evidence that we also grandparent like we were grandparented.[4]

In Figure 2.1, the most striking numbers to me are the "no influence" numbers. It's possible that the Depression and world wars kept our grandparents busy or too numb to be relational. Things were tough. Marriages were strained, but people could not afford to divorce. The suicide rate in the US was at an all-time high in the early 1930s.[5] Twenty-five percent of workers were unemployed in 1933. Hoover was out, FDR was in (four terms he was elected). World War II happened, and many of our grandparents either went to war or stayed home making military items for the war effort. And then came the Baby Boomers (1945–1964). In Figure 2.1, it appears that maternal grandparents were the most influential. This is truer if the child was female.

The message suggested—from Figure 2.1 and the history you have of your own grandparents—is to repeat what was good and do not repeat any bad behaviors or habits. Ask your adult children to hold you accountable if they see you being negative or practicing something bad in front of your grandchildren. Remember, something that you think is normal may not be with your adult children and their children. It may be something that crosses a boundary that may not be clear to you. *Communication is key*. Be open to their wishes. After all, they know what is best for their child. They are the same expert that you were when you had them. The goal here is for your grandchildren to have an owned faith.

---

[4]King and Elder, "The Legacy of Grandparenting," 852.

[5]Feijun Luo, Curtis S. Florence, Miriam Quispe-Agnoli, Lijing Ouyang, and Alexander E. Crosby, "Impact of Business Cycles on US Suicide Rates, 1928–2007," *American Journal of Public Health* 101, no. 6 (2011): 1139–46. https://doi.org/10.2105/AJPH.2010.300010.

Advice from Some Trusted Experts

One of our go-to proponents of intentional intergenerational ministry is John Roberto. John has spent a good part of his life teaching parents, grandparents, and the church community how to come along beside children and teens and disciple them in their faith tradition. In a recent publication he proposed four findings from research that can strengthen parental and family faith practices (which I've listed here with a few edits).[6]

- Parents are the most significant influence on the religious and spiritual outcomes of young people.
- The primary ways by which religious identity becomes rooted in children's lives are the day-to-day religious practices of the family and the ways parents model their faith and share it in conversations, collaboration, and exposure to outside religious opportunities.
- The family is the primary community where religious faith practices are nurtured and practiced.
- The quality of a parent's relationships with their children or teens and the parenting style they practice make a significant difference in faith transmission.

These four items are mentioned so grandparents can purposefully assist their children in sharing their faith story and the great things God has done and is doing in our world.

When you hear about grandparents coming alongside their adult children to help with the grandchildren, you might hear the words "kinship care," "grandfamilies," or "coparents." Good relationships between grandparents and their adult children give the adult children more confidence in their role as a parent and, in turn,

---

[6] John Roberto, "Partnering with Parents to Nurture Family Faith—Insights from Research," *Evangelization & Catechesis* (2020), https://www.usccb.org/news/2020/partnering-parents-nurture-family-faith-insights-research.

their children will be more socially competent. Grandparents, with their rich parenting experience, can provide support, role modeling, and encouragement when they collaborate in raising children.[7]

There are some things parents can do to aid grandparents in being the best coparents possible. Robert Strom and Shirley Strom have developed some goals for teaching grandparents how to better fulfill their role as grandparents.[8] The goals include the following: helping grandparents understand their roles, dealing with difficulties that come with age, giving grandparents needed information, and dealing with satisfactions and frustrations. For example, the authors suggest teaching grandparents about the goals (and boundaries) of the parents for their children so that when the grandparents are with the grandchildren, they are maintaining the same ideals that the parents have set for their children.

Knowing these goals and assisting grandparents with each of them can increase the influence of parents because they are investing not only in their children but in their parents. We know from studies about parent and grandparent relationships that not only does it benefit the grandchildren, but those good relationships can strengthen marriages,[9] which keeps families together.

Grandparents can increase the influence of parents by affirming the parents' actions and beliefs and praising the parents in front of the grandchildren. Joining the parents in faith discussions in the home has a more significant influence on children than

---

[7]Xiaowei Li and Yan Liu, "Parent-Grandparent Coparenting Relationship, Maternal Parenting Self-Efficacy, and Young Children's Social Competence in Chinese Urban Families," *Journal of Child and Family Studies* 28 (2019): 1145–53, https://link.springer.com/article/10.1007/s10826-019-01346-3.

[8]Robert Strom and Shirley Strom, "Building a Theory of Grandparent Development," *The International Journal of Aging and Human Development* 45, no. 4 (1997): 255–86.

[9]Xiaowei Li and Qianqian Liu, "Parent-Grandparent Coparenting Relationship, Marital Conflict, and Parent-Child Relationship in Chinese Parent-Grandparent Coparenting Families," *Children and Youth Service Review* 109 (2020), https://www.sciencedirect.com/science/article/abs/pii/S0190740919309326.

church attendance, Bible reading, and even family prayer time.[10] Other studies show that a father's religiosity is very important.[11] I do Bible journals, emails, and lunches with my two sons. I always encourage them to be the spiritual leader for their families. This is a small way that I can help them to have spiritual influence on their children.

The Grandparent Project study participants were asked how they helped their adult children in material ways (e.g., money, gifts, babysitting, providing transportation, goods) and nonmaterial ways (e.g., ideas, giving advice). Remembering that parents are the greatest influence on their children (for good or bad), we as grandparents want them to have every opportunity to make sure they are a good, positive influence, so many of us go out of our way to give materially and nonmaterially to our children.

How much nonmaterial help (ideas, giving advice) do you provide your children?

	Responses	Percentage
None	8	0.9
Very Little	61	6.7
Some	512	56.7
A Lot	312	34.6
Too Much	10	1.1
Total	903	100

Figure 2.2

Giving advice can be good if it is asked for. We as older people tend to have our opinions, and we don't like change. There is a difference in giving good advice versus our opinion. In the Grandparent

[10] Sarah E. Holmes, "A Qualitative Inquiry into Christian Faith Transmission in the Family Context," *Practical Theology* 16, no. 5 (2023): 604–17.

[11] Lori Baker-Sperry, "Passing On the Faith: The Father's Role in Religious Transmission," *Sociological Focus* 34, no. 2 (2001): 185.

Project study, 91 percent of our participants reported that they give "some" to "a lot" of nonmaterial help. There was not a follow-up question to see if they were sharing ideas or giving good advice.

Be careful giving advice—especially advice that is your opinion. Take every opportunity to affirm your adult children in front of your grandchildren. Commend them for going to church, reading the Bible with their children, praying with their children, and *having open conversations about faith with their children.* As you have opportunities in your home, repeat those same actions and tell your grandchildren how pleased you are with them and their parents for doing the same things in their home.

In Figure 2.3, specifics were not asked as to the type of material wealth given. The figure shows that a little over 80 percent gives "some" or "a lot" of material help to their children.

How much material help (money, babysitting, driving) do you provide your children?

	Responses	Percentage
None	42	4.7
Very Little	117	12.9
Some	397	43.8
A Lot	330	36.4
Too Much	20	2.2
Total	906	100

Figure 2.3

Many grandparents go overboard with giving, especially gifts to the grandchildren. One of our sons has four daughters. They love dolls. We should have bought stock in Mattel. They have sold over one billion Barbie dolls. We have about 50 of those between the four girls. Our son and daughter-in-law finally told us one day that we don't have to buy something for every girl at one of their birthdays (we didn't want the non-birthday girls to feel left out). We also decided together that paying for experiences was better than more Barbie dolls. (We all saved our money in glass jars, and in March 2024 we spent a week in Disney World making memories.) The list below is from our friends at Legacy Coalition[12] on how to be intentional about giving:

- First, ask the parents for gift ideas.
- Know your grandchildren's interests and goals.
- Consider giving experiences rather than tangible gifts.
- Share your artistry and hobbies by giving something you made especially for them.
- Magazine subscriptions are the original "gifts that keep on giving"!
- Other than a cool t-shirt, the gift of clothing may not thrill your grandchild.
- Think about helping your grandchild share a gift with a child in need.
- Surprise your grandchild with thoughtful gifts at other times of the year.
- Give gifts that build memories and impart values.

It is well worth checking out the Legacy Coalition website to get the details of this list. "It is better to give than to receive." Many of us grandparents have that down. I collect eagles (not real ones). I thought it would be cool to get my granddaughters these great big stuffed soft eagles. Guess what? They couldn't care less about eagles. After buying two for my first two granddaughters, that ended. Those two big stuffed eagles are at our house in our family room. Be careful of those things you think are great ideas to buy

[12] Leona Bergstrom, "A Grandparents Guide to Intentional Gift Giving," Legacy Coalition, 2022, https://legacycoalition.com/a-grandparents-guide-to-intentional-gift-giving/.

your grandchildren. They may end up back at your house. (Mine are for sale for two hundred dollars if anyone is interested.)

As you think about giving and receiving from your grandchildren, check out Gary Chapman's five love languages series. He and Ross Campbell authored *The Five Love Languages of Children: The Secret to Loving Children Effectively.*[13] Campbell also authored *The Five Love Languages of Teenagers* for those of you that have older grandchildren.[14] These two resources provide information about Words of Affirmation, Acts of Service, Receiving Gifts, Quality Time, and Physical Touch—the five love languages. According to Chapman, these are the five ways that people receive and express love in all relationships. We are all unique creations. Remember that when you are getting to know your grandchildren. Many wonder how two (or more) children from the same mom and dad can be so different and alike—the beauty of creation!

To close out this chapter, to help your adult children be the best influence on their children (your grandchildren): be a good example, be supportive, know and respect the boundaries, and above all, communicate with them. In the end, the best thing you can do for your grandchildren is support their parents and bless their marriage. (We give our two sons and daughters-in-law two sessions with a counselor every year for Christmas to tune up their marriage. Those sessions are better than another stuffed eagle!)

Reflect and Discuss

1. In what ways were each of your parents influential in your life?
2. Are you able to tell how much influence your grandparents had on your parents? Explain how you saw this in your parents' lives.

[13]Gary Chapman and Ross Campbell, *The Five Love Languages of Children: The Secret to Loving Children Effectively* (Northfield Publishing, 2016).

[14]Gary Chapman, *The Five Love Languages of Teenagers* (Northfield Publishing, 2000).

3. Can you see how much influence you have on your adult children, and are they passing any of your influence down to your grandchildren? What ways do you see that happening?
4. What are some ways that you empower your adult children to be better parents to your grandchildren?
5. Is there any family story in the Bible that your family resembles? How would you relate this story to your grandchildren to make a point about how your faith guided you through the real-life story in your family?
6. Have you asked your adult children specifically how best to support them to be better parents of your grandchildren? Respecting boundaries, how might you point them in different directions without overstepping?
7. This chapter has a list of Scriptures that speak toward raising children. How has the Bible made you a better parent and grandparent?
8. Ron tells the story of redecorating his granddaughter's room and how later that provided a backdrop with mom and daughter to talk about Creation in Genesis. What little things could you do to "plant seeds" that months or years later would connect all three generations (e.g., plant a tree in the backyard together, literally planting seeds)?
9. Discuss ways that you could surround your adult children and your grandchildren with mentors and other disciple-making brothers and sisters who have the same spiritual goals as you. (Especially if you do not live nearby.) The power of the church is that it is universal. You can help make connections of people you trust to influence your children and grandchildren.
10. What is the best piece of advice you would give other grandparents about empowering their adult children to spiritually lead their families?

CHAPTER THREE

Grownup Relationships with Grownup Children

The Parents of Your Grandchildren

"Doing life with your adult children" is a growing phenomenon. Children are moving back home after college, they are getting married later, and they are having kids later. Parents are learning to navigate those waters. Grandparents are learning to negotiate a fine line of boundaries with their children who have children. Issues such as giving advice, overstepping boundaries, supporting children who have left the faith, and relating to children's significant others will be addressed in this chapter.

So, how are your adult children doing in life? We hear things like, "They are finally off the payroll," "launched," "out of the house," and "we are finally empty nesters." There is a part of us that never wants to totally let go. In the end, most of us hope that we gave them good roots and good wings. Most of us want our children to leave (but not too far) and start their own adult lives successfully.

You are probably familiar with the terms "helicopter parenting," "lawnmower parenting," "bulldozer parenting," and "snowplow parenting." These are terms often used to describe overinvolved parenting styles. These labels have been branded on too many parents in the last few years as they attempted to remove obstacles from their children's lives that might cause pain, discomfort, or any type of failure. While it might seem natural for parents to do this, it is not good for children. There is a real world out there with pain, discomfort, and failure. To attempt to remove all negative experiences from your children does not serve your children well as they become adults.

Some parents have taken this to crazy limits. You may recall the college admissions scam in 2019. Several high profile (rich) parents were caught paying money to get their children into top-tier universities. The creator of the college admissions scam was paid twenty-five million dollars from these parents. (You must wonder if your child is not bright enough to get into Stanford, and you buy them a spot, how are they going to pass the classes? Are you going to pay off all their teachers? Where does it end?)

Some believe this phenomenon of overinvolved parenting has been exacerbated by the media. Media blows up one event somewhere in the world and makes it seem to be in all our backyards. In reality, this is one of the safest periods in history to be a child from a violent crime perspective.[1] According to the FBI's violent crime data, violent crimes dropped 10.3 percent in in the first months of 2024.[2] Overprotection robs our children of the opportunities to learn how to solve problems and the struggles that will come up in life. The lack of practice solving real problems can lead to children

[1]Jessica Lahey, *The Gift of Failure: How the Best Parents Learn to Let Go So Their Children Can Succeed* (Harper Publishing, 2016).

[2]Kiara Alfonseca, "Violent Crime Down 10.3% in First Months of 2024: FBI Data," ABC News, October 1, 2024, https://abcnews.go.com/US/violent-crime-103-months-2024-fbi-data/story?id=114380615.

feeling more worried the next time something difficult happens.[3] Back in my youth ministry days, a parent came to me and asked me to write a letter about how their child had been involved in our youth group on service projects and mission trips. This was a required piece of the admissions package for the university she wanted her child to attend. I told her I could not write this letter because her child had never been on a mission trip with our youth group and had never participated in any of our local service projects. I learned a few years later that the mother wrote the letter and turned it in. I'm not sure if she signed my name to it.

You may have been a parent who "gave your children everything." The Grandparent Project survey asked participants questions about how much they help their adult children. As far as giving advice and ideas, 57 percent said they give some, with 35 percent saying they give a lot. When it comes to monetary help, 18 percent said they give little or none to their adult children. Over 80 percent of the sample participants said they give some or a lot of help to their adult children. In addition, participants were asked the same questions about helping their grandchildren. The answers were very similar to the help they give to their adult children.

In a recent survey, parents were asked about their relationships with their adult children.[4] For many, these adult children are the parents of their grandchildren. The list below contains points taken from this study. After this list, I will compare the Grandparent Project study sample with some of these items from the Pew Research study.

---

[3] Meghan Walls, "Parents, Stop Trying to Solve Your Kids' Problems. Their Mental Health Depends on It," USA Today, May 22, 2023, https://www.usatoday.com/story/opinion/voices/2023/05/22/parents-teach-kids-problem-solving-skills/70228030007/.

[4] Rachel Minkin, Kim Parker, Juliana Menasce Horowitz, and Carolina Aragao, "Parents' Relationship with Their Young Adult Children," *Parents, Young Adult Children and the Transition to Adulthood* (Pew Research Center, 2024).

- Roughly 77 percent of the parents reported having excellent or very good relationships with their children.
- The use of technology was high among the respondents of this survey. Some talked every day on the phone. Over 70 percent say they text at least a few times a week.
- The relationships with children who are financially independent from the parent are better than those who still depend on the parents for money or some type of assistance helping with the grandchildren.
- More daughters than sons rely on their parents (especially on mom) for emotional support. Parenting advice was requested by 27 percent of the participants. Jobs and careers were among the highest categories that children sought advice about.
- The group of parents surveyed were more self-reliant than their adult children (51 percent never asked their parents for advice on any topic).
- When it comes to parenting, 40 percent of the participants in this study say they disagree with how their children are raising the grandchildren.
- Concerning religion, 31 percent of the parents disagree with their children's choices about religion.
- When looking at communication, mothers were more often in touch with the children than fathers.

Participants in the Grandparent Project reported very positive relationships with their adult children, over 90 percent saying they have a good relationship. When asked about their relationships with adult children and their spouses, the answers were similar—high quality to very high quality. I followed up with a couple of questions to explore contributing factors to low-quality relationships with adult children, shown in Figure 3.1 below:

	Grandmothers	Grandfathers
Bad feelings from past, not resolved	5%	6%
Different views on raising children	2%	5%
Different political views	3%	3%
Changes in religious views	5%	6%
Financial reasons	1%	1%
Other reasons	9%	10%

Figure 3.1. Factors Contributing to Low-Quality Relationships

The good news is that the percentages are low in the Grandparent Project sample. The participants were allowed to add commentary to the answers above. Some wrote about the bad feelings from the past that they could not resolve, and they were too afraid to ask for outside help. Several mentioned different political views and felt that these different views were also a contributing factor to the changes in religious views of their adult children. Be mindful of things that can cause division in families. Five percent of the Grandparent Project participants reported that their adult children prevented them from seeing their grandchildren.

Connecting with Grandchildren

I asked how grandparents used technology to stay connected to their children and grandchildren. The importance of staying connected cannot be overemphasized. Do whatever it takes to stay connected, especially if you are a long-distance grandparent. Following are ways the grandparents in the Grandparent Project connect to their grandchildren:

How do you keep in touch?	Grandmothers	Grandfathers
Phone calls	68%	70%
Write cards and letters	27%	23%
Send text messages	59%	53%
Send emails	12%	24%
FaceTime	55%	55%
Zoom calls	5%	8%
Go see them	72%	64%
Other	11%	8%

Figure 3.2

When it comes to raising children, there are many experts around telling us how to do it. (These are the people with no children. I was an expert for twelve years until I had children.) I don't recall ever meeting anyone who has or has raised children that called themselves an expert. Most of us learn as we go. We get lots of advice—some of it good—as we move along. You will see the word "boundaries" often in this book. It is a great word if you are the one setting them. It can be frustrating and intimidating if they are set to monitor you.

Only 2 percent of our grandmothers and 5 percent of our grandfathers listed "different views on raising children" as a contributing factor to low-quality relationships with their adult children. Some other factors that may contribute to different views on raising children today could be connected to widespread fears on the Internet (that some grandparents may not be aware of). Problems from the COVID pandemic including depression and other mental health issues are on the rise. Another most recent study by Pew Research lists the greatest worries of our adult children today about their children. Figure 3.3 below is from that study:[5]

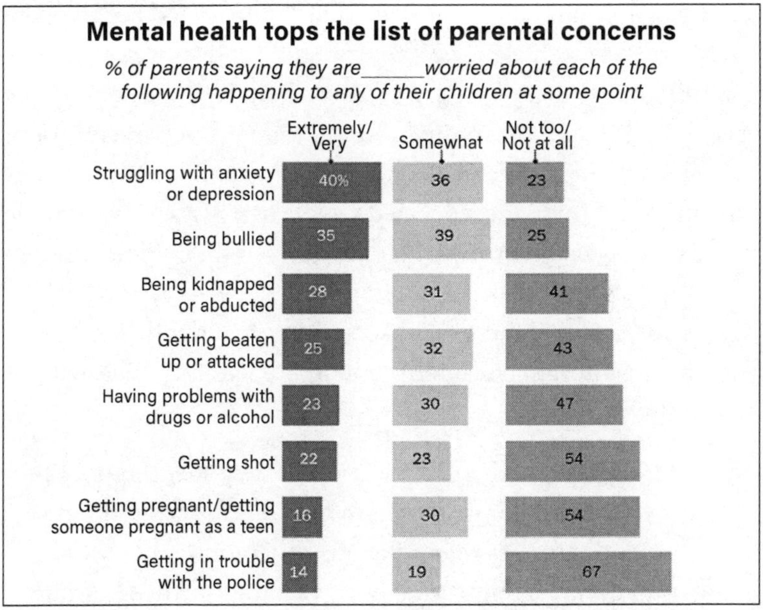

Figure 3.3

Looking back, when most of us grandparents reading this were children in the '50s and '60s, parents' greatest worries were

- Polio (social distancing was practiced)
- Cold War—atomic bomb from Russia; Korean War
- Civil Rights Movement—segregation and desegregation
- Rock 'n Roll music
- Economics
- Radio and television influence
- Cannabis and heroin

---

[5] Rachel Minkin and Juliana Menasce Horowitz, "Parenting in America Today," Pew Research Center, 2023, https://www.pewresearch.org/social-trends/2023/01/24/parenting-in-america-today/.

As I look back, I only remember the first four of these being talked about. Mainly because we didn't have any money, we didn't have a radio or TV, and I did not know what cannabis and heroin were. Every age has its challenges. The Pew study above showed 40 percent of parents disagreeing with how their adult children were raising their children. In our study, at the most 5 percent of our grandparents held different views on raising children. There may be something to a highly educated sample being more aware of the negative aspects of voicing different views to their adult children about how to raise their grandchildren.

As you think about and observe your adult children raising your grandchildren, consider these differences in millennial parenting styles:[6]

- Millennial parents are busier—but they spend more time with their children. Dads are more enthusiastic about parenting duties than previous generations.
- Millennial parents value positive parenting over authoritarian discipline. They are more likely to reinforce positive behaviors than punish negative ones.
- Millennial parents value togetherness (though not always at mealtime). Weekends are key times to be together.
- Millennial parents are (super) safe. They have constant safety information at their fingertips. This can be good and bad.
- Many millennial parents tend to schedule everything—even free time. Families have to carve out "free time."
- Millennial parents understand that these early years are critical and fleeting.

---

[6] KinderCare, "Millennial Parents: Six Surprising Ways They're Raising Kids Differently," *KinderCare* blog, https://www.kindercare.com/content-hub/articles/2016/may/millennial-moms-dads-6-ways-theyre-raising-kids-differently.

Your adult children as parents of your grandchildren aren't so different from the generations before them. They want to love and provide for their kids—in ways that you might not have done for them. Which probably sounds familiar to every parent who has ever had parents "watching" over them.

Participants in the Grandparent Project study were asked several questions about how they parented their children concerning religious practices, specifically church attendance. The participants reported that 77 percent of grandmothers and 81 percent of grandfathers *did not* give their children an option to go or not go to church. I asked later if these same grandparents were satisfied with the church attendance of their adult children now. Only 47 percent of grandmothers and 51 percent of grandfathers answered "yes" to that question. A little over 15 percent of the grandparent participants gave their children an option to go or not go. Within this subset of grandparents, 34 percent of the grandmothers and 41 percent of the grandfathers were not satisfied with their adult children's church attendance. From these numbers, it seems that parents who made their children go to church are less satisfied with their adult children's church attendance compared to those parents who allowed their children the option to go or not go.

The Grandparent Project study participants were asked how often they attended church before and after COVID-19. Research shows that our children will be much like us as parents when it comes to religion and religious practices. It could be that the grandparents in this grandparent study might not be practicing religion as much as one would think, especially with this Grandparent Project being a sample involving mostly churched people. I have over forty-five years of experience working with young people and their families. Many youth ministries were great places for parents to drop off their teens and go back home or go shopping until time to come back and pick them up, instead of attending services themselves. Our children watch us and imitate us in many ways.[7] If church and telling your faith story is not important to you, it will be even less important to your children.

Grandparents in the Grandparent Project were asked if they expected their own parents to share their own faith story with their grandchildren. Over 60 percent said yes. This 60 percent subgroup was asked what their grandparents did that they considered as effective ways to share their faith. They said:

Share your faith story	9%
Be a good Christian example	50%
Spend time with your grandchildren	23%
Be faithful and dedicated to God and church	16%
Be dedicated to family	2%

Next, grandparents in the Grandparent Project were asked how their parents shared their faith with their grandchildren (your adult children now). Grandmothers and grandfathers were very consistent in their replies shown in the list below:

How did your parents pass on faith to your children?	Grandmothers	Grandfathers
Reading the Bible to them	29%	30%
Praying with them	45%	47%
Telling them their faith story	32%	31%
Taking them to church	45%	45%
Teaching them life lessons	54%	46%
Being example on how to treat people	75%	73%
Telling them Jesus loves them	30%	30%
Other	9%	10%

[7]Christian Smith and Melinda Denton, *Soul Searching* (Oxford University Press, 2005).

One of the prayers for this book is that grandparents can be encouraged to verbally tell their faith story. That is, combine all the good things in the lists above with telling your grandchildren verbally your faith story and the great things that God has done and is doing in the world. There is a great little book titled *Saying Is Believing: The Necessity of Testimony in Adolescent Spiritual Development.*[8] The author begs us to say our faith story out loud. Our children and our grandchildren need to hear us say our faith story. People in our churches need to hear us say it out loud. "What we say is who we are." We articulate our identity through story. We often hear this called "giving your testimony." If that word does not work for you and your church, use "faith story." Do something! Stand up and tell what God has done for you and in you.

Our grandchildren need to hear the voices of grandmothers and grandfathers. Mothers and grandmothers have a little more religious influence than fathers and grandfathers. This only means that dads and grandpas need to step it up a notch. My prayer is that both will be bold enough to share their faith story out loud. Be wise and confident. There is more in the chapter for grandmothers and the chapter for grandfathers that hopefully will help you step out and let your grandchildren hear your faith story.

My adult children are a blessing to be around. They don't do everything like we would, but they love Jesus and the church and their spouses and their children—our grandchildren. We have different things we love to do when we are together. Those are sacred times. We love to eat. We love to be outdoors. We love to be together. We pray that you have good relationships with your adult children. Another good book for you is by Dr. Jim Burns, a good friend and brother. The book has a great title: *Doing Life*

[8] Amanda Drury, *Saying Is Believing: The Necessity of Testimony in Adolescent Spiritual Development* (InterVarsity Press, 2015).

with Your Adult Children: Keep Your Mouth Shut and the Welcome Mat Out.[9] Jim does a weekly podcast called *Homeword.* Good stuff.

If your relationships with your adult children are needing a kickstart, I leave you with a list of fun things to do with your adult children (your grandchildren will jump in and join most of these as they get older). There are tons of ideas online, but here are a few to get started. Blessings!

- Host family suppers
- Play Vertellis
- Get out the old photo albums (let your children help you make these digital)
- Play board games (if you are like me, Dudley, do not play Monopoly)
- Create a new tradition (we have *Lord of the Rings* day/night—with some breaks)
- Play "horse" or "21" with a basketball and goal
- Rent a cabin together for a week or weekend
- Go hiking or camping or both
- Do service projects once a month as a family
- Pray together
- Go to church together

Reflect and Discuss

1. What are some things you remember about your grandparents?
2. How did your grandparents affect your faith development?
3. As you think about your adult children, what are you most proud of?

[9] Jim Burns, *Doing Life with Your Adult Children: Keep Your Mouth Shut and the Welcome Mat Out* (Zondervan, 2019).

4. If you have some "fences to mend" with some of your adult children, do so. Ask for help.
5. What ways can you help your adult children be better parents to your grandchildren?
6. Are there some behaviors you need to rein in?
7. Think about the idea of you discipling one or more of your adult children in the faith.
8. Write a note to your adult children and tell them how much you love them.
9. Make sure you understand the boundaries and when to push and when to back off.
10. Share your faith story and the great things God has done and is doing in the world.

CHAPTER FOUR

Styles and Roles of Grandparents

What kind of grandparent are you? What kind do you want to be? This chapter explores the answers grandparents gave in the Grandparent Project study. We are a diverse group of people, with many ways to approach grandparenting. In preparing for the Grandparent Project, I used over fifty books and more than one hundred scholarly journal articles as resources. Within this body of work, the concepts of *styles* and *roles* of grandparents came up often. I thought they deserved a place in this book. How do we grandparent? Where did we learn how to be a grandparent? Do we all have a certain style of grandparenting? Is it cultural? Do different groups of people have certain styles of grandparenting? So many questions.

What is the difference between a style and a role? *Roles* of grandparents are a *specific set of tasks* that have been traditionally carried out by grandparents over the ages (e.g., a caregiver, a substitute for parents, a family anchor). As for *style*, you might think of your grandparenting style as *how you interact with those around you. How you behave. How you influence people and your family. How you carry out the different roles.* Your style probably changes little over time, while the roles of grandparents do change over time. This chapter will provide insight from research and from our study participants about the different styles and roles of grandparenting.

Roles of Grandparenting

Grandparents in the early 1900s in the USA had different roles than the grandparents I surveyed in the Grandparent Project. Grandfathers appeared to be invisible and at best "hovering and inactive in the shadow of grandmothers."[1] Recent studies show as men age, they become more compassionate.[2] This makes them available for roles that formerly were allocated to grandmothers. For years, grandfathers' roles were seen as secondary compared to the nursing and caring roles of grandmothers. This seems to be changing. Grandfathers do have a softer side. This may be partly due to getting older, but also grandfathers seem to be stepping up to more of an active mentoring role in the lives of their grandchildren. Grandparents are living longer. Most have more time than ever in their lives, time that they probably did not spend with their own children because of work. Some are redeeming that time and spending it proactively with their grandchildren. Grandfathers have more *available* time.[3]

There are many options grandparents can take (or are forced to take) when deciding what their role will be as a grandparent in the family. Over half of our participants in our grandparent

---

[1]Ann Buchanan and Anna Rotkirch, *Grandfathers: Global Perspectives* (Macmillan Publishers, 2016), 74.

[2]Barbara R. Tinsley and Ross D. Parke, "Grandparents as Support and Socialization Agents," in *Beyond the Dyad*, ed. Michael Lewis (Plenum Press, 1984), 161–94.

[3]Buchanan and Rotkirch, *Grandfathers*, 75, 86.

study said that distance was the number one reason they could not be present with their grandchildren. Thirty percent of our 995 study participants are still working full-time. It is refreshing to see that many of our grandparents have learned other ways to be in touch with their grandchildren using electronics. These high-tech grandparents are not letting distance, or in some cases their own children, keep them from staying in touch with their grandchildren. Ten years ago, we never imagined that one of the roles of grandparenting would be played out using technology.

All grandparents have an image of the perfect grandparent shaped by their own experiences and their faith and values. The following four-step process is suggested to craft a vision for the role of grandparent that you want to live out:[4]

- Reflect on your own experiences as a grandchild and how they have shaped you.
- Think about your stand on some of the key aspects of grandparenting.
- Consult with your adult children during the process.
- Describe your vision.

This process has everything to do with presence (*being there*), traditions, family values, boundaries, financial gifts and assistance, and relationships with other family members. Have a set vision for your role as a grandparent. As your grandchildren grow older, the vision for your role may need adjustments. Stay in touch and be intentional.

Forty years ago, grandparent studies were highlighting the absence of grandparents.[5] It was reported that the roles of

---

[4]Peggy Edwards and Mary Jane Sterne, *Intentional Grandparenting* (Fulcrum Publishing, 2008), 17.

[5]Arthur Kornhaber and Kenneth L. Woodward, *Grandparents/Grandchildren: The Vital Connection* (Transaction Publishers, 1991).

grandparents had been replaced by babysitters, television, restaurants, therapists, celebrities, and youth culture in general. Many grandparents felt powerless, role-less, disconnected, and replaced. It is not easy to tell whether grandparents abdicated the roles, or if they were pushed out of the roles. Probably some of both. In the Grandparent Project, over 50 percent of our participants see their grandchildren one or more times a week and are intentionally involved in their lives. These participants are serious about the role they are playing in the lives of their grandchildren.

Staying connected is a big deal. When writing this chapter, I ran across this idea that it was our fault as grandparents for not staying close—as in relationships (and, I would argue, proximity). We have given up places where grandparents used to be, like front porches and attics. Front porches are where you learn the stories. The attics are where all your grandparents' treasures are (for some of us it may be the garage or the shed out back). I love it when our grandchildren come over. They love to explore our closets and upstairs bedrooms. I don't think they have been in the attic yet. They find little things that are pretty worthless to anyone else but become little treasures for them. We intentionally "plant" some of this stuff for them to find and keep. They learn some stories about us connected to those little treasures. Passing on stories and treasures about us as grandparents is big. We know that those are important for the preservation of our family history, but we also know that telling our faith story and the great things God has done and is doing in our world is bigger. That role is the most important role for all of us grandparents.

In line with our study of telling our faith story and the great things God has done and is doing in our world, Tim Kimmel describes four roles grandparents can carry out as spiritual leaders for their grandchildren:

Blessing Giver. As Blessing Givers, grandparents can provide (1) *spiritual blessings* by praying with and for their grandchildren regularly and modeling God's unconditional love and value for them; (2) *emotional blessings* by encouraging their interests and gifts, pointing out the ways in which God has uniquely designed them, sharing in their achievements, and comforting them in time of discouragement; and (3) *relational blessings* by providing an environment where they are unconditionally accepted and protected.

Legacy Builder. As Legacy Builders, grandparents can pass along to their grandchildren (1) *an honorable legacy* by living a life of integrity, responsibility, and selflessness; (2) *an instructive legacy* by modeling the truth through example and finding teachable moments to speak truth into their lives; and (3) *an eternal legacy* by demonstrating faithful obedience to God and having a Kingdom-sized vision for life.

Standard Setter. As Standard Setters, grandparents can invest in the personal character and values of their grandchildren by nurturing in them a biblical worldview through example and personal instruction. Six areas in which grandparents can set the standard for their grandchildren are: *faith, integrity, poise, discipline, endurance, and courage.*

Torch Bearer. As Torch Bearers, grandparents can help guide their grandchildren toward a missional lifestyle through (1) *evangelistic fervor* by sharing the gospel with them, showing interest in their growth in Christ, and demonstrating concern for lost people through words and action, and (2) *righteous clarity* by helping them understand how to be in the

> world but not of the world and providing wisdom for living a godly and grace-filled life.[6]

In connection with our grandparent study, I surveyed and interviewed several college students, asking them about the roles that their grandparents played in their lives. Their answers mirrored several that were found in the books and articles used as sources for this study. Roles like that of *historian, hero, mentor, role model, nurturer, and wizard.*[7] Most of these roles require grandparents to *be present* in the lives of their grandchildren. Listen to our college students talking about the presence of their grandparents:

> My grandma is the most religious person in my family. She made me go to church all the time with her which made me go to church and learn about God now.
>
> Growing up I would stay at my grandma's house on weekends, and we would always go to church on Sundays. She would read me her favorite books of the Bible and send me verses every day to keep me involved with the church while I was busy at college.
>
> My grandmother helped me grow spiritually because she told me her faith story. How she had been through a lot in her life and how she finally came to Jesus.
>
> My grandmother always told me stories about the Bible and would tell me without Jesus we wouldn't have eternal life.
>
> My nanny helped me grow spiritually by staying up with me and reading me Bible stories. She lives with me now and is unable to drive. The effort she puts into going to church every Sunday and

[6] Tim Kimmel and Darcy Kimmel, *Extreme Grandparenting* (Focus on the Family, 2007), 79–146.

[7] Kornhaber and Woodward, *Grandparents/Grandchildren*, 168–79.

Wednesday is very inspirational to me. I think most people would just not try. That continues to show me how devoted she is, and I enjoy taking her to church often.

My grandpa baptized me. He is one of my biggest mentors. I model my faith after him.

My grandpa was an elder in our church and constantly encouraged me in my spiritual life. Something that stuck with me was how he taught me to talk to the newcomers at church and show them God's love.

My granddad took me to church every Sunday and Wednesday. He prayed with us a lot.

My grandfather would sit with all his grandkids in front of him and we would play his question game. All the questions were from the Bible. For every answer we got right we got a dollar. He's the reason I read the Bible without being asked to.

My grandmother helped me grow a lot spiritually. She would sing songs about Jesus around the house. She would also read the Bible out loud to me. She's the one who told me about being baptized and what it meant.

Grandparents, do not underestimate the importance of you *being there*. Arthur Kornhaber points out the importance of grandparents telling their faith story:

> The potential for spiritual resonance between the young and the old explains why spiritual teachings, embodied in the world's religions, are most easily passed on from grandparent to grandchild. Many grandchildren observe their grandparents involved in spiritual activities—going to a place of

> worship, keeping religious traditions at home, demonstrating reverence for nature, espousing spiritually based values and principles. Indeed, grandchildren often see their grandparents as "guardians" of spirituality and religious faith.[8]

As grandparents, we must not give up that special role of telling our faith story and the great things God has done and is doing in our world.

Styles of Grandparenting

You might think of your grandparenting style as how you interact with those around you. How you behave. How you influence people and your family. How you carry out the different roles you have. Your grandparenting style is more of a collection of behaviors that represent how you approach and carry out the grandparent role. For example, I am a risk-taker. My life verse comes from John 10:10: Jesus came that I might have life and have it to the full. I am grabbing on to everything I can. I am living life to the full. That gets me into situations sometimes that might have been better if I had sat and thought about it more. But my style is to go get it and help as many other people get it along the way—especially getting Jesus. Nothing else really matters in the long run.

Some researchers explore grandparenting styles in three different categories: remote, companionate, and involved.[9] *Remote* relationships often refer to not being present because of physical distance. It can also mean emotionally remote, which happens when grandparents become disconnected or estranged from their families due to divorce, in-laws, daughter-in-law problems, political differences, and even religious differences. We found all of these to be true for some of our grandparent participants. Keep

[8] Arthur Kornhaber, *Contemporary Grandparenting* (Sage Publishing, 1996), 102.
[9] Andrew Cherlin and Frank Furstenberg, *The New American Grandparent* (Harvard University Press, 1992).

in mind that 99 percent of our participants are church people. Church people are not immune to negative life events. The difference for most people facing these events is the way they cope. In our study, most grandparents who talked about bad things that happened in their lives and their family got through these times because of their faith. This is a great opportunity for us grandparents to share with our grandchildren about how God and our faith are walking us through trying times.

Companionate relationships are the most dominate style of relationships with most grandparents and grandchildren. This style of grandparenting is often characterized as doing emotionally satisfying leisure-time activities with your grandchildren. Grandparents tend to be very easygoing and friendly. This type of grandparent usually doesn't worry about being in the role of parent. They are around to give out all the extra love that they now have (that they many times did not have for their own children because of work and other parental duties). Most grandparents are okay with not being the boss. Most grandparents are aware of the very powerful "norm of noninterference"[10] between them and their adult children. Grandparents interfering in the way their children are raising their children is seen as one of the worst sins a grandparent can commit. Be careful.

The *involved* style of grandparenting is almost an exact opposite of the previous two styles. The involved grandparent is more like the parent of the grandchildren. They are in daily contact. Most have been forced into this style of grandparenting due to divorce, death, substance abuse, and other unexpected events. In the grandparent study sample of grandparents, 73 grandparent families have grandchildren living with them for a variety of reasons that will be discussed more in Chapter Six.

---

[10] Cherlin and Furstenberg, *New American Grandparent*, 57.

As early as 1964, research on grandparents discovered five styles of grandparenting: *formal, fun seeker, surrogate parent, reservoir of family wisdom,* and the *distant figure.*[11] In 1977 a research study on grandmothers produced four styles of grandparenting: *apportioned, symbolic, individualized,* and *remote.*[12] In 1986 five grandparenting styles emerged from the research: *detached, passive, supportive, authoritative,* and *influential.*[13] In 2002 research uncovered five distinct grandparenting styles: *influential, supportive, authority-oriented, passive,* and *detached.*[14] Specifically looking at grandfather styles, in 2012 researchers classified grandfathers as *involved, passive,* or *disengaged.*[15] More involved grandfathers had better health.

Most of the terms in the paragraph above are self-explanatory. If you have been grandparenting long, you probably can see yourself in one particular style or maybe some combination of styles. Grandparents come in all shapes and sizes. The way they do grandparenting has a lot to do with how it was done to them and how life has treated them. Certain personalities will lean toward certain styles. The idea here in this chapter is awareness. If you lean toward styles like passive, detached, or remote, you may have to put forth some extra effort to become influential and supportive.

I grew up working very hard. I have a very strong work ethic. I do not have much room for people who are lazy and not willing to share the load. I noticed that with my granddaughters I started

---

[11] Bernice L. Neugarten and Karol K. Weinstein, "The Changing American Grandparent," *Journal of Marriage and the Family* 26, no. 2 (1964): 199–204.

[12] Joan F. Robertson, "Grandmotherhood: A Study of Role Conceptions," *Journal of Marriage and Family* 39, no. 1 (1977): 165–74.

[13] Andrew J. Cherlin and Frank F. Furstenberg Jr, *Styles and Strategies of Grandparenting: A Place in the Family, a Life Apart* (Basic Books, 1986).

[14] Margaret M. Mueller, Brenda Wilhelm, and Glenn H. Elder Jr, "Variations in Grandparenting," *Research on Aging* 24, no. 3 (2002): 360–88.

[15] James S. Bates and Alan C. Taylor, Grandfather Involvement and Aging Men's Mental Health," *American Journal of Men's Health* 6, no. 3 (2012): 229–39.

out very tough with them. It might have worked better with boys, but it does not work well with girls. So my prayer has been for this year to be more compassionate. I did a study on this word in the Bible, and guess who would look at people and have compassion on them? Jesus. I really do want to be more like him. I want my grandchildren to see Christ in me. I want to be an influence in their lives so that when I tell them my faith story and the great things God has done and is doing in our world, they will listen and learn.

Focusing on the telling of our faith story, different styles grandparents use to influence their grandchildren's faith development have been discussed by Bengtson. In his studies of grandparents and faith, he has discovered four styles or ways that grandparents have *religious influence* with their grandchildren:[16]

- **The "Skipped Generation" Influence: Grandparents Substituting for Parents.** Grandparents' influence on their grandchildren's religious lives is so extensive that they serve as replacement figures for the children's parents.
- **Grandparents Reinforcing or Enhancing Parents' Religious Influence.** This is the good one. The adult children and grandchildren share the same religious tradition and beliefs as the grandparents. This is grandparent–parent mutual reinforcement. This is the ideal scenario for passing on the faith.
- **Grandparents Challenging or Subverting Parental Religious Socialization.** This style of influence has many negative consequences for families. Grandparents attempt to force their beliefs and traditions on their

[16] Vern Bengtson, *Families and Faith: How Religion Is Passed Down across Generations* (Oxford University Press, 2013), 105–12.

grandchildren when this goes against the implicit or explicit wishes of the children's parents.

- **Grandparents Ignoring Grandchildren's Religious Socialization.** This style doesn't cause overt negative consequences, but grandparents tend to be indifferent, noninterfering, or ambivalent. They simply are not involved at all in the spiritual lives of their grandchildren.

Finally, other researchers combine styles and roles into what they call "types of grandparents."[17] They offer the following to choose from. (Which are you?)

- **The Enforcer. Rules are rules.** Someone has to keep things in order.
- **The Spoiler**. You do all the fun parts of parenting without the responsibility, arguments, and guilt. Your favorite word is *yes*.
- **The Executive**. Your career is the most important thing for you. You only make time for grandchildren when it fits your busy schedule.
- **The Globetrotter**. You retire and set off to see the world. Having grandchildren is not going to stop you. You think you are a good example to them about reaching out and taking all that you can—without them in your way.
- **The Environmentalist**. You are all about saving the whales and not cutting down trees and getting rid of plastic. You must save the earth and pass that on to your grandchildren's generation.
- **The Buddy**. You are on a first-name basis with your grandchildren. You are super cool. You know all their lingo, movies, and music. You are cool.

[17] Georgia Witkin, *The Modern Grandparent's Handbook* (Penguin Books, 2012).

- Other honorable mention types were **the Pushover, the Cuddler, the Coach,** and **the Counselor.**

In the grandparent study, we did not specifically ask grandparents what style or role they play in their grandchildren's lives. We did ask some questions that hint at what some of the styles mentioned above might be. For example, participants were asked, "How do you feel about the following statement: Grandparents have the authority over the parents to guide their grandchildren on their perspectives of right and wrong?" Figure 4.1 depicts how our sample felt about that question. Grandmothers and grandfathers are pretty much in agreement on this question. Only 8 percent of our participants agreed or strongly agreed that they should have authority over the parents of their grandchildren on matters of right and wrong. These particular grandparents might be classified as the *enforcer, challenging and subverting, or* authority-oriented types, as mentioned above. It is also interesting that of the 8 percent, they were highly educated (having a bachelor's or master's degree).

It is not surprising that over 50 percent of our participants disagreed or strongly disagreed with that statement. Most grandparents today do not want to interfere with their children's child-rearing decisions. As you think about the type of grandparent you want to be, be careful to honor the boundaries that your children have set for their children. This can be difficult when your children aren't doing anything of a spiritual nature with your grandchildren.

We followed up this question with two other questions that were testing the parent-child boundaries of our grandparent participants. These two questions were directed more toward the religious aspect using the element of prayer. We asked our participants to agree or disagree with the following two statements:

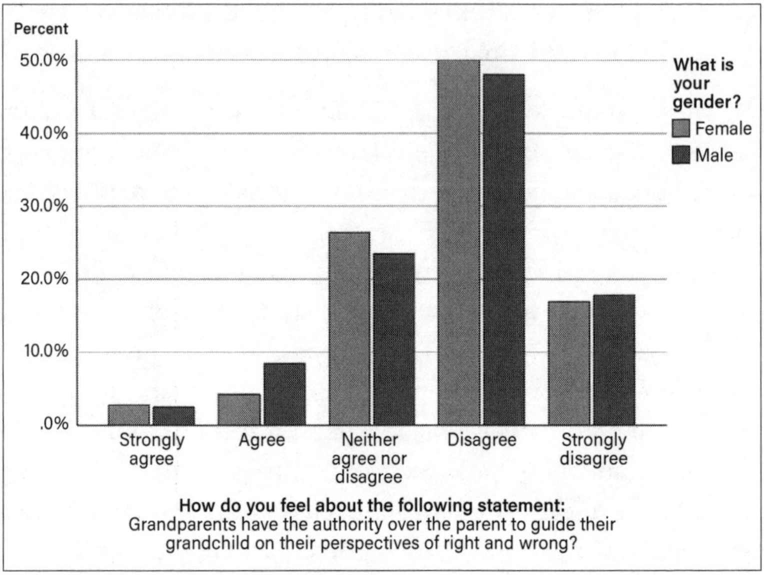

Figure 4.1

"Grandparents should require/insist on prayers of thanks before meals and bedtime when the grandchildren come to visit," and "Grandparents should require/insist on prayers of thanks before meals and bedtime when they are visiting their grandchildren in their homes." It has been pointed out by participants that if you "require or insist" on anything, you should have a conversation about what you mean and why it is so important to you. Today's grandchildren have Google. They can get more information than they need. Showing and explaining how to use the information wisely provides grandparents more opportunities to build relationships with their grandchildren.

In the Grandparent Project, it was interesting to find that grandfathers agree and strongly agree more than grandmothers about prayer in their home. Looking at our chapter on grandfathers, this could be an example of the compassionate side or softer side of men as they age. As much as most of us would agree that prayer is important, make sure you know, understand, and follow the boundaries your children have set up for their children. Life will be smoother. In the case where some of you feel that more prayer is needed, pick and choose wisely other times to stress that importance to your grandchildren. In fact, teach and model to your grandchildren how important prayer is to *you*, so that when they are in their home, it becomes natural for them to suggest and say prayers.

The list below gives insight into what the college students who were interviewed remember about prayer from their grandparents.

- She is always telling me she is praying for me. She is one of the main reasons why I believe.
- She would read me stories of Jesus and encouraged me to pray before my meals.
- When I stayed at her house we prayed together. She shared her journey stories, and we worshiped together.
- She takes me to church and tells me stories of the gospel and prays with me.
- He prayed before every meal.
- He prayed with us a lot.
- My grandpa always was the one to pray at the dinner table. He made sure we never forgot to pray.

Whatever your role or style of grandparenting is, make sure that the basis of it is the spiritual—to tell your grandchildren the great things God has done and is doing in our world. I would also tell you that you must tell your grandchildren your faith story. As I had video calls with several adult grandchildren this past month, I was amazed at the legacy that being a servant, being a faithful churchgoer, having good marriages, and being good to the grandchildren had on these grandchildren. They recalled all these things about their grandparents. Not one of them that I interviewed had been told the faith story of any of their grandparents by their grandparents. You must do this! They will not forget you telling them over and over about how you became a follower of Jesus and that you continue to follow every day. And as a reminder, your number one grandparent job is to support your children as they rear their children—your grandchildren. Help them be the heroes of your grandchildren.

Reflect and Discuss

1. Think about your grandparents. What style of grandparenting did you observe in them?
2. What roles did your grandparents play?
3. Think about the style of grandparent you are. What is something you need to work on to be a better grandparent?
4. What roles do you carry out with your grandchildren?
5. Do you have different roles with your different grandchildren? What are their ages and genders, and what do you do different with each one?
6. We know that some of you are probably rearing your grandchildren full-time. (God bless you!) What differences have you noticed in you rearing your grandchildren versus the way you reared your children?
7. We saw differences between grandmothers and grandfathers throughout our study. Is there anything connected with grandparenting that you and your spouse need to get on the same page about?
8. Do not be too proud or afraid to ask for help with a role that you see coming up in the lives of your grandchildren. What might be one of those you see in the future to work on?
9. What type of prayer person are you?
10. Make a list of things to pray about daily for your grandchildren. Give them a list of things to pray about for you.

CHAPTER FIVE

Health and Well-Being of Grandparents

I taught a gerontology course in university for a few years. We covered many aspects of aging. I would pair my students up with folks in a nearby assisted living facility. They hated it at first, but by the end of the semester, lasting friendships would result for several students that would continue even after the course was over. Health was a big topic in the course. Students could see first-hand the health status of many of the residents in the assisted living facility. I would have insurance people come to class and talk about long-term health care policies. Doctors would come and talk about health. We would spend at least two sessions talking about dementia and the outcomes families faced with a loved one going through mental health issues. I covered chronic diseases in two or three sessions because of the urgency and increase of these diseases in many older people's lives.

After WWII, there were several advances and improvements in our country's overall health. Unfortunately, as the baby boomer generation reached the grandparenting age, we began to see a decline in population health in our country. Several research studies have confirmed this downward trend.[1] Heart disease, strokes, cancer, and diabetes are the major chronic diseases in North America. People are more at risk if they smoke, eat poorly, drink too much alcohol, and do not exercise. Doctors report that as many as six in ten adults in the United States have a chronic disease, and four in ten have two or more chronic diseases.[2] Studies have also shown that people use religion and spirituality as a coping mechanism for their chronic illnesses.[3]

The participants in the Grandparent Project study were asked several questions about their mental and physical health. When asked if any life events affected their faith development in a negative way, they gave the following answers: suicide, addictions, alcoholic spouse, COVID-19, mental health issues, trauma, rape or sexual assault, identity issues, autism, ALS, death, same-sex attraction, disabled children, and exhaustion from taking care of aging in-laws, to name a few.

Poor health was one reason given preventing grandparents from having access to their grandchildren (5 percent of our grandmothers and 5 percent of our grandfathers). About half of the participants in the grandparent study reported their health as high quality to very high quality (18 percent to 48 percent for grandmothers and 18 percent to 52 percent for grandfathers). Only 7 percent of our grandparents said that their health prevented them from spending more time with their grandchildren. There were

---

[1]Hui Zheng, Jonathan Dirlam, Yoonyoung Choi, and Linda George, "Understanding the Health Decline of Americans in Boomers to Millennials," *Social Science and Medicine* 337 (November 2023), https://doi.org/10.1016/j.socscimed.2023.116282.

[2]AARP, "Health," *Policy Book*, https://policybook.aarp.org/policy-book/health.

[3]A. Elizabeth Rippentrop, "A Review of the Role of Religion and Spirituality in Chronic Pain Populations," *Rehabilitation Psychology* 50, no. 3 (2005): 278–84.

four questions in our survey centering on health that we eventually used in a composite scale to get scores on our participants' overall outlook on life. An interesting aspect of the table below is the differences in scores between grandmothers and grandfathers who chose "agree" or "strongly agree" to answer the four statements.

Survey Item	Grandmothers	Grandfathers
These are the best years of my life	49%	55%
I feel old and somewhat tired	36%	33%
I worry and can't sleep sometimes	26%	15%
Life is hard much of the time	9%	6%

So does grandparenting improve health?[4] Nonresiding grandparents have better health than grandparents raising grandchildren in their homes and grandparents living with their children and grandchildren. As noted in our chapter on grandparents raising grandchildren, 73 of the Grandparent Project participants did not have a choice to be nonresiding. Comparing these 73 grandparents with the rest of the 995 participants, I found that their reported health status in the category of "high quality" to "very high quality" was 60 percent compared to the higher score of 68 percent for our nonresiding grandparents. Our group of grandparents raising grandchildren scores lower on every measure of health and health-related questions that we asked. Being a parent again definitely takes a toll.

Thinking about the category of nonresiding grandparents, which 92 percent of the grandparent study participants fall into, the following comes from a study of grandparents and health connected to their grandchildren:

---

[4]Mirkka Danielsbacka, Lenka Krenkova, and Antti O. Tanskanen, "Grandparenting, Health, and Well-being: A Systematic Literature Review," *European Journal of Ageing* 19, no. 3 (2022): 341–68.

> Grandparents often have close relationships with their grandchildren, and those relationships often change when a grandparent becomes ill. Physical health and illness influence how grandparents and grandchildren interact. When healthy, grandparents are often more involved physically in the lives of their grandchildren. When grandparents are affected by chronic illness, their interactions with grandchildren may become limited or, at least, changed. In some cases, grandchildren may step in as caregivers for their grandparents. When grandparents contract terminal illnesses or are in the active process of dying, grandparents and grandchildren can experience a poignant closeness that often leaves lasting impressions on grandchildren. Even after the death of a grandparent, grandchildren often carry a legacy from their grandparents in their hearts.[5]

In reference to the declining health and passing of grandparents, the college students I interviewed said things like:

> My nanny helped me grow spiritually by staying up with me and reading me Bible stories. She lives with me now and she is unable to drive. The effort she puts into finding a ride to church every Sunday and Wednesday is very inspirational to me. I think most people would just not try. That continues to show me how devoted she is, and I enjoy taking her to church often.

> My father's mother took me to church every Sunday along with my parents from the moment I was born until she passed away a year ago. She had so much faith and led by example and I still look up to her.

[5] Jeremy B. Yorgason and Melanie S. Hill, "Grandparents and Health," in *Grandparenting: Influences on the Dynamics of Family Relationships*, ed. Bert Hayslip Jr. and Christine A. Fruhauf (Springer Publishing, 2019), 201–16.

> My father's mother is a living example that our bodies are a temple, and if taken care of we can continue teaching as long as we live. Seriously, she cannot die.
>
> My father's father helped me grow spiritually by relating the Bible to my sports and the struggles I would go through. Ever since my grandma passed away, it is evident to me that the thing that keeps him going is the hope of the Resurrection.

These college students focused on the spirituality of their grandparents. They saw and felt the good even in death. Family relations are a big deal. Grandchildren do not automatically know how to value their elderly people. They learn to do that by being around their grandparents. Grandparents should enjoy all the stages of development their grandchildren go through. And do not be too scared of the teenage years. Grandchildren passing through adolescence may appear to distance themselves from their grandparents. Don't feel too bad—they are distancing themselves from their parents also. If you have had a good, close relationship with them up until the teens, most will come back around.

There is a concept called "intergenerational solidarity."[6] Six factors from this concept can help grandparents have a closer bond with their grandchildren, which can increase life expectancy and better health.

- **Physical Proximity to Grandchildren**—We knew this. The closer you live to your grandchildren, the easier it is to be close. In our study of grandparents, distance was the number one reason given for not being around as much as they wanted to. I have had several grandparents tell me that they packed it all up, sold the house, and

---

[6] Vern L. Bengtson and Robert E. L. Roberts, "Intergenerational Solidarity in Aging Families: An Example of Formal Theory Construction," *Journal of Marriage and Family* 53, no. 4 (1991): 856–70.

moved to where their children lived and worked just to be closer to their grandchildren. You may not be able to do that. Don't forget about technology. Learn how to use FaceTime and Zoom.

- **Frequency of Contact with Grandchildren**—Obviously, the more you see your grandchildren, the more likely you will bond closer. (This becomes a setback with parental divorce. If there is not joint custody, it can get nasty.)
- **Grandparents' Role within the Family**—Refer back to Chapter Four on styles and roles. We can surmise that our 73 grandparents raising grandchildren are closer to their grandchildren than the other participants in our study. The opportunities to bond are almost 24-7. *Presence* is important. Take advantage of all the times you get to be with your grandchildren.
- **Family Expectations**—Research studies show that families that expect strong relationships between the generations are more likely to have them. These families come to the table often. They teach loyalty and unconditional love for all members of the family.
- **Emotional Bonding with Grandchildren**—Don't be mad or confused when you realize that your grandchildren love their parents more than you. That is the way it is supposed to be. Make sure you are supporting the parents! As we age, we will notice that our friends are beginning to come down with some of these chronic diseases and that some of them are already passing on. This makes some grandparents become clingy. Don't smother your grandchildren to meet your own emotional needs. Be close and support your children—this will bring you closer to your grandchildren.

- **Reaching a Consensus on Values**—Families are closer when they share the same values. I asked our study participants how important it was to carry on family traditions. Over 87 percent "agreed" or "strongly agreed" that this was important. More than 90 percent said they had taught some of their skills to their grandchildren.

I am a big proponent of intentional intergenerational ministry. I have co-taught a graduate class and at conferences about why universities ought to be teaching intentional intergenerational ministry.[7] Grandparents can help build that intergenerational solidarity best by supporting the parents as they raise their children. We know that intergenerational relationships between grandparents and their grandchildren benefit the health of both. These relationships can do the following:[8]

- **Encourage Physical Activity**—Spending time with your grandchildren doing activities helps your blood pressure, weight loss, and strength and flexibility. This also gets your grandchildren away from screens.
- **Improve Mental Health**—Having strong relationships with grandchildren significantly decreases the risk of depression for both. Exchanging skills, ideas, and your faith story can help boost self-esteem.
- **Extend Life Expectancy**—The more you hang out with your grandchildren (even occasionally) the better your health will be. The less social you are in general, the greater the chance of you developing chronic health

[7] Association of Youth Ministry Educator's Conference, 2013. https://www.aymeducators.org/wp-content/uploads/AYME-Booklet-Final-2013-1.pdf.

[8] Raymond Hobbs, "How Kids and Seniors Can Keep Each Other Healthy," MI Blue Daily, September 9, 2023, https://www.mibluesperspectives.com/stories/family-health/how-kids-and-seniors-can-keep-each-other-healthy.

conditions. Play with your grandchildren, go to church, and hang out with your neighbors.

- **Provide Emotional Support**—Research shows that grandchildren who have a close relationship with grandparents are less likely to have behavioral or emotional problems. We as grandparents can be a great support system. Especially when your grandchildren become teens. If you have built a good relationship with them, and they need some advice that they don't want to ask their parents about, they might come to you. Be careful not to create an "us against the parents" scenario. Watch those boundaries.
- **Set a Positive Example**—You as a grandparent have the opportunity very early on to present a healthy lifestyle to your grandchildren. They are watching you. A positive example is important. More than 87 percent of the grandparent study participants said they are a good example of loving God and others in front of their grandchildren.
- **Teach Practical Skills**—Your grandchildren have learned that if they want to know anything, they can Google it. Technology is not all bad, but you will never know how good camping and hiking are until you go do it. You can watch people make clothes, but grandmothers teaching granddaughters how to sew is invaluable. You can watch all the videos on how to hit a golf shot. There is nothing better than to go play golf with your children and grandchildren. (They will learn a lot about you when watching how you handle a golf club.) Again, more than 90 percent of the participants in our study said they had taught some of their skills to their grandchildren.

There is an innovative place in London, England, where children help elderly people live longer. Nightingale House is one of the first residential homes for the elderly that has an on-site nursery.[9] Two- to three-year-old children interact daily with the residents. Activities they enjoy together include baking, gardening, art, and exercise. Thinking about mental and physical health, residents and staff at Nightingale had these comments about being intergenerational:

> "When the children come in, they recognize you after some time, and now I have all these adopted grandchildren and great-grandchildren." —Garcia

> "I see (Garcia) move round and round the building walking, going to different places," he said. "That's physical exercise with a purpose, because she's got somewhere to go, and she's got something that she's doing, which is different from trying to motivate herself." —Simon

> "People are becoming more and more aware of the age apartheid that we live with. . . . We're not learning from each other. Very small children are very nonjudgmental. They're very accepting, and they're also very interested and very creative. They see things often from rather quirky directions." —Judith

> "[Residents] very often forget their own physical limitations, and they find that they are encouraged; they stretch themselves; they will lean up out of their chair, extend a hand, and engage in conversation. . . . The residents enjoy watching the

---

[9] "New London Care Home Champions Intergenerational Care," Nightingale Hammerson, May 12, 2021, https://nightingalehammerson.org/news/article-title-in-full-5/. Meera Senthilingam, "Intergenerational Care: Where Kids Help the Elderly Live Longer," CNN.com, February 16, 2018, https://www.cnn.com/2018/02/16/health/longevity-intergenerational-care-elderly-children-intl/index.html.

children and observing them. They engage different parts of their brains." —Ali

The directors of this Nightingale project are seeing positive results in residents that include reduced depression, increased mobility, better communication and language, and lower levels of dementia and memory loss. We know that connecting generations is associated with lower levels of dementia, depression, and high blood pressure and stronger immune systems, and most of us are just happier when we are around children, especially our own grandchildren. At a time when older people are more alone, children can bring a sense of value, hope, and joy to older people. We are also helping children when we are together. We can teach them skills, give them wisdom, and most importantly, share our faith story and the great things God has done and is doing in our world.

Are You Centenarian Material?

Health is a bigger deal as we get older. If you watch TV at night on MeTV, four out of five commercials are pointed at the older generations. It seems if you bought everything they are advertising, you would live forever. And just in case you might think you could die, Joe Namath will sell you some term life insurance, and Tom Selleck will reverse mortgage your home so you can pay for the insurance premiums.

Do you want to live to be one hundred? Learn about the Blue Zones.[10] I learned about these zones when I was teaching gerontology. These are areas in the world (Ikaria, Greece; Loma Linda, California; Sardinia, Italy; Okinawa, Japan; and Nicoya, Costa Rica) where populations live to be over one hundred years old, mostly because of their diet. Studies have been done in these zones

[10] www.bluezones.com.

to discover why the people live longer. The Blue Zones researcher found that food has a lot to do with longevity but also close family ties and faith. It's another reason to be sharing your faith story and telling others about the great things God has done and is doing in our world. The Blue Zones researcher found nine common denominators (lifestyle habits) that people in these five areas around the world displayed:

- **Move Naturally**—They move without thinking. They grow gardens. They do not have mechanical conveniences.
- **Purpose**—Don't quit when you retire. Find a new purpose in life. Blue zones people know why they wake up in the morning.
- **Downshift**—Even people in the Blue Zones experience stress. Stress leads to chronic inflammation, which is associated with every major age-related disease. What the world's longest-lived people have that we don't have are routines to shed that stress. Okinawans take a few moments each day to remember their ancestors, Adventists pray, Ikarians take a nap, and Sardinians do happy hour.
- **80 Percent Rule**—Okinawans stop eating when their stomachs are 80 percent full. The 20 percent gap is the difference between losing weight or gaining weight. Eat your smallest meal in the afternoon and nothing else the rest of the day.
- **Plant Slant**—Beans are the cornerstone of most centenarian diets. They on average only eat meat about five times a month (serving size about the size of a deck of playing cards).

- **Wine at Five** (maybe Welch's grape juice for some of us)—All Blue Zones people drink one to two glasses of wine per day. The key is to drink it with friends and food.
- **Belong**—The Blue Zones researcher interviewed 263 centenarians. All but five of these belonged to a faith-based community. Attending church could add four to fourteen years of life expectancy. (Who knew?)
- **Loved Ones First**—Successful centenarians put their families first. Keep grandparents in your home or very nearby. It increases the life of children, also.
- **Right Tribe**—The centenarians in the Blue Zones chose or were born into circles that supported healthy behaviors. For example, Okinawans created "moais"—groups of five friends that committed to each other for life. (If you watch the original Blue Zones documentary, you will meet some of these groups. It is amazing watching these five friends over one hundred years old each sitting around talking about life and family.)

I really think the last one here (right tribe) is so important. Good research shows that getting out of the house and being social increases your life expectancy. Your tribe might be your golfing group, your quilting group, your Bible study group, your book of the month group, any group that you meet with on a regular basis and have some accountability. Accountability and commitment to the group is the key for the "moais" found in the Blue Zones. Today, it seems that even our groups of special friends may only be superficial at best. Spend time developing strong, lasting friendship groups. Our immediate family is one of those important groups. Make sure you are doing everything in your power to make the parents of your grandchildren the leaders of your grandchildren. This will endear you to both and will be healthy.

Other possible indicators of quality of mental and physical health were explored with the Grandparent Project study participants. Seventeen questions that were later combined into four indexes measuring the overall attitude of our participants were asked. The four factors that emerged from the responses were positive outlook on life, negative outlook on life, future outlook on life, and not worried outlook on life. The following displays the scores from our participants:

Outlook on Life
(Scores range from Strongly Agree to Strongly Disagree—1–5)

Positive Outlook on Life	2.7 out of 5 (Smaller is better)
Negative Outlook on Life	3.8 out of 5 (Larger is better)
Future Outlook on Life	2.3 out of 5 (Smaller is better)
Not Worried Outlook on Life	2.7 out of 5 (Smaller is better)

We know that negative attitudes affect physical and mental health.[11] Having good relationships with our children and grandchildren gives purpose and meaning. How a person looks at life can be a factor in their longevity. Studies show that people with positive attitudes live more than seven years longer than people who have negative attitudes. Being satisfied with your life and having confidence in you are also great predictors of a longer expectancy of life. New research is coming out that suggests a person's mindset—how they feel about growing old—may predict how much longer and how well they live as the years go by.[12] The

[11] "Discrimination and Negative Attitudes about Ageing Are Bad for Your Health," World Health Organization, September 29, 2016, https://www.who.int/news/item/29-09-2016-discrimination-and-negative-attitudes-about-ageing-are-bad-for-your-health.

[12] Julia Nakamura, Joanna Hong, and Jacqui Smith, "Associations between Satisfaction with Aging and Health and Well-being Outcomes among Older US Adults," *JAMA Network Open* 5, no. 2 (2022), https://jamanetwork.com/journals/jamanetworkopen/fullarticle/2788853.

study suggests the following for older people to develop a more positive approach to aging:

- Maintain a sense of purpose (take your grandchildren out and plant a tree in the park)
- Recognize negative messages about aging—and reject them (don't be a victim of ageism)
- Stay socially active (go to church instead of watching online; be with people)
- Try something new (learning new skills helps memory and overall quality of life)

As a grandparent, you have a tremendous opportunity to share life-on-life with your grandchildren. Your ideas, insight, skill sets, and attitudes are so important for the development of children. In my opinion, you have the privilege of sharing your faith story and the great things that God has done and is doing in our world. Stay as healthy as you can for your grandchildren's benefit.

Reflect and Discuss

1. Discuss what you know about heart disease, strokes, cancer, and diabetes. Why do you think they are the major chronic diseases in North America?
2. What are you doing to fight these diseases in your and your family's life?
3. Have you experienced times when you physically could not do an activity with your grandchildren? What did you do instead?
4. What touches you or moves you the most from reading the comments from college students about their grandparents? Do these comments give ideas as to what you might want to add or change in your life as it pertains to influencing your grandchildren? What would you add or change?

5. How does your church or civic organization deal with intentional intergenerationality? What are some specific things they do? If they are not doing this, what would you suggest for them to do to become more intentional?
6. What were your thoughts when you read about the Nightingale House in London? Have you experienced a place like this where you live? What are some things you could do to help an assisted living business become more intergenerational?
7. Please put this book down and go watch the Blue Zones documentary on Netflix.
8. What do you think of the nine lifestyle habits that Dan Buettner discovered about the five Blue Zones? Which ones are you already doing? Which ones do you need to try?
9. The idea of the "moais" groups from Okinawa is intriguing. It reminds me of the discipleship that we read about in the early church. Selling everything so that no one has a need. Having all things in common. Laughing together, crying together, dying together. Lots of accountability and commitment.
10. If you are wondering about the outlook on life scores and how you did or would do, you can do a quick little check in the back of the book with the seventeen questions in the Appendix and see where you come out. The whole idea here is to be as positive a person as you can be. It helps you and it makes us like you more. Your grandchildren will like you more.

CHAPTER SIX

Grandparents Raising Grandchildren

Parents Again

Grandfamilies. Kinship care. Possibly new words and phrases for some of us. Remember the song "Age of Aquarius"? We are now in the "Age of Grandparenting." In times past, grandparents and elderly died in place, usually in the old home place or with one of their children—we took care of them. Now in our North American culture, many of our elderly go to assisted living homes or nursing homes as they age.

There is a growing group of our grandparents and elderly that is being called upon to be "parents again." The US Census Bureau reports about 6.7 million people lived with their grandchildren in 2021. (This report was released March 19, 2024.) Over 32 percent of these grandparents are responsible for the total care of their grandchildren. Numbers are higher across the South and Southwest. For example, Oklahoma is in that group. Eastern counties in Oklahoma have higher than average numbers of grandchildren living with grandparents. Figure 6.1 below from the Census Bureau shows the different ages of the children that some grandparents are taking care of.

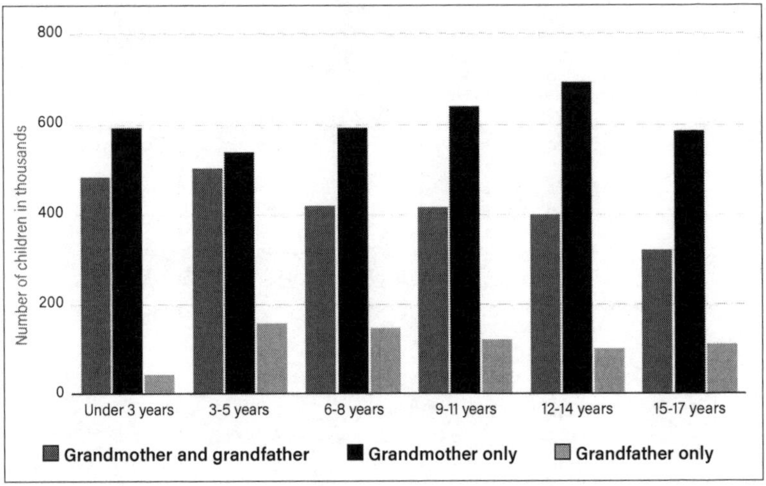

Figure 6.1

Seventy-three participants in the Grandparent Project were currently taking care of and raising their grandchildren. While the grandparent study sample was comprised mostly of Caucasian participants, based on census data we expected to find more Hispanic (13 percent national average) and African American (40 percent national average) grandparents living with grandchildren. This was not the case. Sixty-eight of those seventy-three participants were Caucasian.

Another assumption made based on national statistics was that these families would be on the lower side of the income category. Not so with the Grandparent Project sample. Figure 6.2 shows the exact opposite of that assumption. Almost 70 percent of our 73 grandparents raising grandchildren report income from $50,000 to over $150,000. Only 8 percent of these grandparents could be reported as at or below the poverty level. The national average is 21 percent below the poverty level for grandparents raising grandchildren.

Valid	Frequency	Percent	Valid Percent	Cumulative Percent
Under $15,000	2	2.7	2.7	2.7
Between $15,000 and $29,999	4	5.5	5.5	8.2
Between $30,000 and $49,999	6	8.2	8.2	16.4
Between $50,000 and $74,999	12	16.4	16.4	32.9
Between $75,000 and $99,999	15	20.5	20.5	53.4
Between $100,000 and $150,000	28	38.4	38.4	91.8
Over $150,000	6	8.2	8.2	100.0
Total	73	100.0	100.0	

a. Are any of the children or grandchildren you have listed above currently living with you? = Yes

Figure 6.2

Several grandparents that I spoke with in person or on Zoom who were raising grandchildren in their homes were not thrilled 100 percent to be doing that. The increasing trend in grandparents raising grandchildren is due to:

- increasing numbers of single-parent families
- deportation of parents due to immigration issues
- the high rate of divorce
- teenage pregnancies
- incarceration of parents
- substance abuse by parents
- illness, disability, or death of parents
- parental abuse or neglect[1]

[1] "Grandparents Raising Grandchildren," American Academy of Child and Adolescent Psychiatry, April 2017, https://www.aacap.org/AACAP/Families_and_Youth/Facts_for_Families/FFF-Guide/Grandparents-Raising-Grandchildren-077.aspx.

One researcher discusses the "four Ds" (divorce, desertion, drugs, and death) as reasons for the increase.[2] The increase in this phenomenon has led lawmakers to introduce bills such as S.1091—Supporting Grandparents Raising Grandchildren[3] and recently bill S.3501—Grandfamilies Act of 2023.[4] Many people entering the grandparent age are generally about ready to retire or slow down and enjoy some of the benefits of their lifelong labor. To be thrown back into raising children is not their idea of retirement. Research shows that giving that up and taking over the responsibilities of being a primary caregiver again can stir up many feelings, including grief, anger, loss, resentment, and possibly guilt. The transition can be very stressful, and the emotional and financial burdens can be significant.[5]

Good social science research shows that children being raised by grandparents, other kin, or the foster system have challenges emotionally, behaviorally, physically, and academically. Good news for grandparents raising grandchildren: Your grandchildren you are raising do better in these challenges than children in foster homes. Other studies show that children raised by grandparents can turn out to be relatively healthy and well-adjusted.[6] Younger children raised by positive grandparents will have greater success in school compared to children who do not have good relationships with their caregivers. Younger grandparents, especially resentful younger grandparents, tend to spend less time providing

---

[2]Rachel Dunifon, "The Influence of Grandparents on the Lives of Children and Adolescents," *Child Development Perspectives* 7, no. 1 (2013): 55–60.

[3]Introduced by Senator Susan Collins of Maine (2017).

[4]Introduced by Senator Robert Casey of Pennsylvania (2023).

[5]"Grandparents Raising Grandchildren."

[6]Oliver W. Edwards and Andrew P. Daire, "School-Age Children Raised by Their Grandparents: Problems and Solutions," *Journal of Instructional Psychology* 33, no. 2 (2006): 113–19.

educational support for their grandchildren. Most younger grandparents are still working full-time. Almost half of the grandparents raising grandchildren in the Grandparent Project are still working full-time (see Figure 6.3).

Some Hispanic grandparents in our survey were raising their grandchildren. These households faced unique challenges because in some cases only one member of the family spoke English well. If your grandchildren were learning English, imagine how challenging it would be to help them with homework. How would you support your grandchildren if they were learning a language that you didn't grow up speaking?

Another challenge for grandparents raising grandchildren that I was reminded of from working with teens so many years was the generation gap. When I dealt with the "generation gap," it was about the differences between the parents and the teens. Think about the differences between children in today's culture and their grandparents' generation. It was difficult enough trying to bridge one gap. Think of the challenge to bridge two. If a grandparent takes on babies and small children, there may not be much of a transition. If a grandparent suddenly has a teenager in the house, it could be a challenge. A challenge with discipline, technology, and even health care. Attempting to discipline a teen who has not had much discipline could be a disaster. Grandparents are at a disadvantage to help with homework and other school projects as the education system adopts more technology and requires students to use that technology. One study referenced in this book project discussed outdated health care methods that grandparents raising grandchildren were using (e.g., leaving wounds open instead of applying clean bandages, putting children in ice to reduce fever, putting butter and ice on burns).[7] The challenges leave many of these grandparents in desperate need of assistance.

As grandparents, most of us want to be involved in the lives of our grandchildren. We want to be influential in their lives. We want to leave some type of legacy. Many of us have heard people say, "Skip children, go straight to grandchildren." This almost happens to grandparents raising grandchildren. They end up skipping part of their lives to raise grandchildren. In a previous chapter, we discussed the different roles and styles of grandparents. When it comes to grandparents raising grandchildren, three different, specific roles surface:

- Day-care grandparents, who provide regular, daily care for an extended period.
- Living-with grandparents, who reside with a grandchild but do not have legal custody (usually the grandchild lives in the grandparent's home).
- Custodial grandparents, who have obtained legal responsibility for the grandchild.

There are different challenges specific to each of these additional roles put on grandparents raising grandchildren. Adjustments and changes must be made. Many of these changes do not come easily. One study from North Dakota State University reported the following about the role adjustments of grandparents raising grandchildren:

- **Attitude adjustment—**Grandparents usually anticipate later life as a time to enjoy the privileges of grandchildren without

[7] Ludivine Brunissen, Eli Rapoport, Kate Fruitman, Andrew Adesman, "Parenting Challenges of Grandparents Raising Grandchildren: Discipline, Child Education, Technology Use, and Outdated Health Beliefs," *GrandFamilies: The Contemporary Journal of Research, Practice and Policy* 6, no. 1 (2020), https://scholarworks.wmich.edu/grandfamilies/vol6/iss1/6.

many responsibilities. Adjusting to the new role of primary caregiver typically takes some effort. Also, it may mean many adjustments in life planning, from finances to career changes to location and lifestyle changes.

- **Mixed feelings—**Most adults enjoy being grandparents and associating with grandchildren. However, taking on the role of raising a grandchild can bring mixed feelings because grandparents feel increased anxiety and pressure while also appreciating closeness to a grandchild.
- **Sense of purpose—**Grandparents involved in raising grandchildren often report a greater sense of purpose in their own lives. While the change may not be expected, most grandparents raising grandchildren describe a greater sense of purpose in life because of their caretaking responsibility.
- **Heightened stress—**Raising children brings with it common stresses, from meeting basic needs to making sure homework gets done. Often, grandparents raising a grandchild experience significantly more stress than other caregivers due to such things as financial concerns, physical limitations, or adjusting to transitions. Grandparents in this role need support in caring for their own physical and emotional health.
- **Need for support—**The support needs of grandparents raising grandchildren often increase. Providing for education costs, medical needs of children, discipline and guidance, and other tasks requires support and encouragement from others.[8]

We asked the grandparents raising grandchildren in the grandparent study some questions to see how they were currently

---

[8]Divya Saxena and Sean Brotherson, "When Grandparents Become Parents to Their Grandchildren," North Dakota State University Extension Office, revised March 2021, https://www.ndsu.edu/agriculture/extension/publications/when-grandparents-become-parents-their-grandchildren.

adjusting to life in general. Figure 6.3 compares our grandparents raising grandchildren to the other grandparents in our study who are not raising their grandchildren.

Survey Item	GPs Raising GC		GP NOT Raising GC
GP is most important thing in your life	53% SA/A		41% SA/A
Did not raise my kids right. . . .	25% Yes		8%
Grew up in HH with both parents	80% Yes		89% Yes
Employment	44% Full T		29% Full T
	11% Part T		8% Part T
	40% Ret		59% Ret
Education			
Less than four years of college	48%		32%
Graduated from college	23%		33%
Masters	16%		23%
PhD, MD, DD, DO	2%		7%
Health Quality	60%	VHQ to HQ	68%
Positive Outlook on Life	2.715	Smaller is better	2.4/5
Negative Outlook on Life	3.8/5	Larger is better	4.0/5
Future Outlook on Life	2.3/5	Smaller is better	2.1/5
Not Worried Outlook on Life	2.7/5	Smaller is better	2.8/5
Income			
Under $15,000	3%		0.60%
$15,000 to $29,999	6%		4%

Survey Item	GPs Raising GC		GP NOT Raising GC
$50,000 to $74,999	16%		11%
$75,000 to $99,999	21%		21%
$100,000 to $150,000	38%		23%
Over $150,000	8%		19%

Figure 6.3

All of the grandparents in the Grandparent Project were asked if grandparenting was the most important thing in their lives. For grandparents raising grandchildren, 53 percent agreed or strongly agreed with this statement versus only 41 percent of grandparents not raising grandchildren. This may be explained simply by the fact that for grandparents raising grandchildren, those duties fill their lives compared to other grandparents who have time to "have a life."

The second item on the table above is about second chances. Many sermons and several books have been written about "the God of second chances." And we certainly get that because of what Jesus Christ has done for the world. The fact is, we get second, third, fourth chances. Seventy times seven. Some grandparents believe they get a second chance to get it right with their grandchildren. This is bad psychology and theology, however, and whatever you did with your children is done. If a person feels this way, I propose they probably need forgiveness, not a second chance. In the grandparent study, 25 percent of our grandparents raising grandchildren said they saw raising their grandchildren as a second chance to get it right versus only 8 percent of our grandparents not raising grandchildren. If you look back at the list of reasons for the increasing trend in grandparents raising grandchildren, it is easy to see why some of these grandparents might feel guilty for not raising their children right. Parents get and take much of the blame and shame when their kids turn out badly. Some of it may be their fault, but there are so many other variables to raising children that may have affected the outcomes of parenting.

Most of the other variables in the table are similar for both groups. The grandparents raising grandchildren are a little less educated, have more full-time workers, and are as well-off financially as the grandparents not raising grandchildren. The health quality and outlook on life are similar for both groups. As grandparents live longer than ever, it is predicted that this trend of grandparents raising grandchildren will continue to grow and last longer. They need help.

Support for Grandparents Raising Grandchildren

Many of our grandparents raising grandchildren are doing okay financially and may not need extra monetary help and support. The demands placed on grandparents raising grandchildren can be diverse. Regardless of a grandparent's age, race or ethnicity, gender, living situation, or economic status, all grandparents raising grandchildren have a need for education and support. Just knowing how to get in touch with social service agencies and support organizations, or a child custody special lawyer, is a good start for many. Some healthcare and nonprofit organizations offer grandparenting classes to address the changing roles of grandparents. Some churches have support groups for grandparents raising grandchildren. One predominately African American church in my city has a grandparent support group that meets once a week. These and other support groups can assist grandparents raising grandchildren in some of the following areas:

- Legal assistance for custody or guardianship
- Financial assistance (welfare, Medicaid, Medicare)

- Assistance with housing and utilities
- Help with school enrollment and transfers
- Counseling or therapy options
- Information on local support groups

Support groups and services for grandparents raising grandchildren are becoming nationally recognized (e.g., Legacycoalition.com, Aarp.org, Christiangrandparenting.com, Focusonthefamily.com, Intentionalgrandparenting.com, Acl.gov, Helpguide.org). These support groups can provide networks and connections to specific resources and partners in your city and state. Several states and university extension programs offer PASTA (Parenting A Second Time Around). It is usually free and is for grandparents raising grandchildren and other caregivers' support.

A Final Word

If you think parenting your own children was demanding and stressful, parenting again in the grandparent age can be doubly daunting. This second time around (not a second chance) does give grandparents raising grandchildren a platform that many other grandparents do not have: daily time to tell your faith story (much through modeling) and time to talk about the great things God has done and is doing in our world. Grandparents raising grandchildren have an opportunity to make lemonade out of lemons. Many of the 73 grandparents raising grandchildren in the grandparent study were doing so.

Grandparents are very important and influential people to grandchildren of all ages. If you are a grandparent raising a grandchild, please read or reread our chapter on styles and roles and adjust your new role. Do not be afraid to ask for help. If there is not a support group at your church, start one. If you are into technology, start an Internet group or join one that specializes in grandparents raising grandchildren. Please remember this: The child is not responsible for the situation you have been thrust into. *Do not blame them.* Be careful not to add more negatives to their lives. Surround them with good people—and you be good people. Grandparents raising grandchildren have extra opportunities to guide their grandchildren physically, mentally, and most importantly, spiritually.

Reflections and Discussion (for grandparents raising grandchildren)

1. What is your greatest struggle? What is your greatest need?
2. If there is not a support group in your area, start one. Check out the support groups and resources listed in this chapter.
3. What suggestions do you have that could help others?
4. How has your church helped you in raising your grandchildren?
5. Do not be afraid to seek counseling and therapy. Contact AAMFT (aamft.org) to find a counselor or therapist in your area who specializes in working with grandparents raising grandchildren.
6. Have you asked your grandchildren for help with things like school and technology? Were they willing to help you?
7. Look back up at the section in this chapter on role adjustments. If you are having some challenges adjusting, please ask for help.
8. In all that you are doing, don't forget that they are watching you. It is important that you be present for them. It is important that you be a person of faith in front of them. Are there areas concerning faith, religion, or church that you need help with? Once again, please call on your local church for help.
9. If you are having immigration challenges, reach out to some locals. There are lawyers that are willing to help. In my city (Oklahoma

City) the Catholic Charities Archdiocese of OKC provides immigration legal services. There are probably similar services in other large cities in the United States.

10. We have heard good things about the PASTA program. Check your local extension services and take advantage of this help.

CHAPTER SEVEN

The Importance of Grandmothers

Interviewer: If your grandchildren asked you to tell them the story of your walk with God, how would you tell that story?

Grandmother: I talk to my grandchildren all the time about how important it is to walk with God. And talk to him about whatever problem you have. If they can be able to voice or think and tell God their troubles, it can lift a burden from their shoulders, so I try to tell them that on whatever level they are. And, of course, every time my grandchildren come visit they always want to come into my class. I don't care if they are two and I'm teaching five-year-olds, three, four, eighteen . . . they want to come into my class. And I always let them come into my class. Number one, I want them to see me teaching children as an example; number two, they learn. There are things they learn in there. They may learn

> how to teach, but they may learn something about the Bible that they never heard. And number three, I love having them with me.[1]

This grandmother felt that conversations about faith were a part of her mission in life, not only with her grandchildren but with the other children who came into her Bible class Sunday after Sunday. She was confident in the story she told and in her ability to tell it. As compelling as her words are, our research led us to discover that many grandmothers are neither as vocal about their faith nor as confident in their voices. How do grandmothers talk about their faith? What are the habits that convince their children and grandchildren that they are people of faith? This chapter explores these questions.

For years, we have been studying how families talk about faith. One of our larger projects has been the Three Generations Study,[2] which found common intergenerational factors in faith sharing within the Churches of Christ. We conducted our research by conversing with families that have stayed in that fellowship for three or more generations.[3] We used interviews and other qualitative research methods to find out how faith-resilient families adapted to changing circumstances and stressors from generation to generation. These conversations have given us insights into how

---

[1]Special thanks to Dr. Ron Bruner for writing this chapter, combining previous research with this current grandparent study. Names in this chapter have been changed to maintain anonymity. Respondent F2G2P1F, interview, Three Generations Study. Hereinafter, we refer to the respondents by their code number. Any names or locations in the comments have been changed to protect the privacy of the families involved. The code numbers empowered the researchers to identify the generation, gender, and number of each respondent without using their name.

[2]Portions of this chapter and the methodology for the Three Generations Study can be found in Ron Bruner and Dudley Chancey, "A Line of Matriarchs: Findings from the Three Generations Project," *Discernment: Theology and the Practice of Ministry* 10, no. 1 (2024): 13–30, https://digitalcommons.acu.edu/discernment/vol10/iss1/2/.

[3]This study was reviewed and approved by the University Research Board at Oklahoma Christian University on February 6, 2012.

such families have grown together in faith. In all three generations, everyone we talked with (1) was willing to participate in this study, (2) was an adult with the liberty to make choices about where and whether to pursue their faith, and (3) had adequate possession of their faculties of recall and communication.

In Churches of Christ, we found that families steadily loyal to that faith family for three or more generations often had a chain of matriarchs who kept their family connected to that faith family. Although researchers note the importance of fathers and grandfathers as an important factor (and it *is* one important factor), we found that spiritual matriarchs can be as effective in nurturing a healthy family faith in the long term. To show this, we will describe how families have constructed roles and negotiated tasks in ways that are more practical than theological. In many cases, mothers have handled certain spiritual roles and tasks in the family because of parental time commitments and the division of childcare responsibilities. This tendency has shifted in recent generations as marital partners have newly negotiated solutions.[4] Thus, in this area, leadership by mothers and grandmothers has been a practical response to perceived needs.

Secondly, spiritual mothers and grandmothers have provided intergenerational familial spiritual leadership. Some of these grandmothers may not be as vocal as the grandmother quoted at the beginning of this chapter, but they are no less committed in how they live. Consequently, we will talk about day-to-day faith practices that often historically involved women more than men, while noting that current generations are changing role expectations. The family stories we have heard show that women often make key choices whether to stand firm within their faith group or to yield previously held ground to maintain family solidarity

---

[4]For a broader discussion of the shift in spiritual roles in families, see Penny Edgell, *Religion and Family in a Changing Society* (Princeton University Press, 2006).

and continuity. Some grandmothers defend conservative doctrinal positions to maintain a connection with the mainstream beliefs of the faith group. Other grandmothers flexibly adjust their doctrinal boundaries to keep younger generations in their circle, even though those younger family members hold beliefs that are unorthodox, but not central, to the identity of the faith community. For many grandmothers, the nurture and wholeness of their church community are key to their understanding of their faith.

Not only did we find a surprising number of matriarchs present in the group of families that participated in our study, but in many cases, these matriarchs form a chain that spans as many as five generations. These lines of matriarchs were the spiritual backbone in families of various types, keeping this role even when strong male leaders (deacons, elders, or ministers) emerged within or married into the family.

In this chapter, we use the word *matriarch* to describe a woman (usually older) who is the head of a family or exercises significant power within a family. A *patriarch* is a man (usually older) who is the head of a family or exercises significant power within a family. In differing cultures, either or both can be normative. In this work, we use the terms descriptively without saying that either role is necessarily bad. We do recognize that the term patriarchy is deeply problematic because it presumes fixed gender roles, including male leadership and female submission, and too-frequent abuse of power.

What We Found

In Churches of Christ, certain spiritual practices are preferred ways to form children as members of this faith group. In our qualitative study, prayer, Bible study, attending worship, living moral lives, and talking about faith are, in the opinion of the respondents, central spiritual practices for families within this faith group. In our more recent quantitative study, we asked grandmothers what they thought was important in sharing faith with their grandchildren (see Figure 7.1).

Practices Grandmothers Believe Important for Sharing Faith

Practice	Percent
Be good Christian examples	51.1
Spend time with grandchildren	19.7
Faithful and dedicated to God and the church	17.6
Share their faith	10.2
Dedicated to family	1.4
Total	100.0

Figure 7.1

In many ways, what our quantitative study found grandparents believe to be important aligns with what works according to our qualitative study. "Be good Christian examples" equals "live moral lives," "share their faith" aligns with "talking about faith," and "faithful and dedicated to God and the church" is close to "attending worship." Yet grandmothers in our quantitative study did not mention Bible study and prayer, whereas families in our qualitative work identified both as core practices of faithful families. It is important to understand that the things we believe to be important do not always line up with the most successful practices. Because our qualitative work describes practices that we found among our families who have successfully carried faith across several generations, this chapter will present our conversations with those families to explore how women, especially grandmothers, have walked alongside their children and grandchildren in lives of faith.

The Practice of Prayer and Bible Study

In considering the spiritual discipline of prayer, people in our study recall two recurring prayer times prominent in their lives as children: mealtime and bedtime. Among the respondents in this study, fathers are almost universally the parents who lead prayer at the dinner table. When asked about their first memories of prayer, respondents would typically recall memories as did this generation-two mother about her generation-one matriarch:

> R: It would have to be at mealtime and when we went to bed at night. Mother would tuck me in and say prayers. That's the earliest I remember.
>
> Q: Who typically did the praying at mealtime?
>
> R: My dad.[5]

In a very similar way, generation three of the same family recalls being parented by her generation-two mother and father:

> Q: What are the earliest memories you have of prayer in your family?
>
> R: Um, I think mine would be sitting around the table at dinner, with my dad. My dad was always the one that led the prayer, and we did it at every meal. That's what I remember the earliest.[6]

The habits of who leads prayers at certain times and in certain settings tends to carry from one generation to the next.

Many other families had similar experiences. Another generation-two daughter remembers "praying with my mom at bedtime when I was a little girl and praying at the dinner table."[7] At

---

[5] F19G2P1F, interview. See also F25G2P1F, interview.
[6] F19G3P1F, interview.
[7] F15G2P1F, interview.

meals, fathers or grandfathers typically led prayers. When fathers were present but did not lead the prayer, they usually decided who led the prayer, whether by naming the leader, asking for volunteers, or taking turns.[8] "At dinnertime—we would take turns as to who would pray. But my mom never prayed. It was always me, or my brothers, or my dad who prayed."[9]

When grandfathers were present in their own homes, they might lead or choose the leader. When asked whether anyone else besides her grandfather led prayer at her grandparents' home, one woman responded:

> R: It was always Grandpa.
>
> Q: Do you remember how he prayed?
>
> R: It was very detailed . . . and it just went on and on until Grandma squeezed his hand telling him to quit. Then [*laughing*] it was "Amen."[10]

The prayers of grandparents can be especially endearing to grandchildren when they speak of the relationship between their grandparents.

> Q: What are the earliest memories you have of prayer in your family?
>
> A: Some of the earliest memories that I have are praying before meals with my immediate family. Then the other memory that I have, one of my fondest memories is praying before the dinner table but with my grandparents—both sides—but particularly I remember my father's father praying at the dinner table and he'd say, "We thank thee, our heavenly Father" and he'd also pray at the end for his wife who was in a nursing

[8] F22G3P1M, interview.
[9] F8G3P1F, interview.
[10] F45G3P1F, interview.

> home and he'd pray "Dear Lord, when You take her from this sweet earth, I pray that she will just fall asleep and You will take her." And so I remember how sweet and how sincere his prayers were. And when I was a teenager that is exactly how my grandmother passed away so that was pretty profound for me at that age. To remember those memories of prayer.[11]

Mothers may also teach their children how to pray, yet they typically do so as a part of bedtime prayers. This is also often when Bible study is mentioned. One generation-two mother recalls, "My earliest memories of prayer are of my mother, praying with me at bedtime. At first, she read a prayer out of a children's book, but as time went on, I began to say my own prayers."[12] Her son received his understanding of prayer from her in a similar way: "As far back as I can remember, my mom would sit down with my brother and I and read us a story out of the *Children's Story Bible*, then after that, we would pray together."[13] Others had similar experiences.

> Q: What are other times of family prayer that you remember?
>
> R: My mom used to tuck me in at bedtime and said prayer. It didn't happen every night, but I remember very vaguely of her reading a story to me and saying a prayer before I went to bed.[14]

Ultimately, this generation-three mother describes her prayer practice with the fourth generation: "I read her Bible every night to her. After we read the Bible, we talk about the story that we just read again. We always end with praying for our family and our

[11] F2G3P1F, interview.
[12] F10G2P1F, interview.
[13] F10G3P1F, interview.
[14] F19G3P1F, interview. See also F22G2P1M, interview.

friends. At the dinner table, we say the same prayer every night, and she's almost saying it on her own now."[15] It is important to see that the spiritual parenting practices of the grandparents shape the parenting practices of the next generation with their children (and the grandparent's grandchildren). *As mothers walk alongside their children in faith, they are often already shaping how they will be seen as grandparents.* Childhood memories endure, sometimes to be imitated, sometimes to be transformed.

A generation-one woman whose father was not converted until later in her life noted that prayers happened at "bedtime mainly because my dad was never home at mealtime. He worked different hours, so we ate before he got home and were in bed before he got home."[16] Sometimes this learning process happened without mothers ever actually having prayed in front of their children. As a matter of fact, some generation-two and generation-three respondents observed that they had never heard their mothers pray, even though they were fully aware that this was their regular practice.

When grandmothers have grandchildren as guests in their homes, or when they are guests in their grandchildren's homes, they may have the opportunity to model these prayer practices with yet another generation. Spending time with grandchildren in this way affirms the model that the parents present and connects the story of all these generations to the ongoing story of God in this world. "As for us and our house, we will serve the Lord."

Prayer practices, though, are changing over time for various reasons: attitudes in the church, individual attitudes, and personal temperament, for example. There is clear evidence in this study of shifting attitudes about the roles of men and women in the family,

---

[15] F19G3P1F, interview.

[16] F19G1P1F, interview.

and in the practices of new generations of parents.[17] Consider this exchange with a generation-three parent who is working through her experience with her parents (her daughter's grandparents) in teaching her daughter to pray:

> R: At the dinner table, we say the same prayer every night, and she's almost saying it on her own now. We want to teach her to be open about praying because, [with] me growing up, it wasn't like that.
>
> Q: What do you mean by that?
>
> R: My dad was always the one that said the prayer, so I was never in a position that I had to. And, you know, when I got married, Matt was in a family where he grew up that his mom said the prayer a lot, and when we would pray, he would ask me to pray, and I wouldn't do it. I feel like prayer is a very personal thing to me. I struggle to pray in front of people because I don't want to sound dumb. I don't want to sound like I don't know what I'm talking about. I want to teach Lauren that it is okay to pray out loud. That it is okay to pray in front of other people because I was scared about doing it. One year we had Small Groups, and after Bible Study, we did a big chain prayer, and every night, I would get nervous and get sick to my stomach because I don't know how. I still struggle with how to pray. Do I just talk like he's there? Do I have to get formal? I want Lauren and Hanna to feel like it's okay to pray openly and not be scared to do it.

[17] Although this shift may have been emerging for some time, it has been more operant and less publicly espoused in some faith groups. W. Bradford Wilcox, *Soft Patriarchs, New Men: How Christianity Shapes Fathers and Husbands* (University of Chicago Press, 2004).

> Q: Do you feel like your dad being the only one that prayed has hindered you from being open about praying? Looking back, how do you feel about that? What are your thoughts on that?
>
> R: I'm not. I'm a shy person when it comes to being in front of people. So even if I had the opportunity to do it more, I don't know if I would do it. I'm just a private person. Very quiet. I really struggle with when I'm on the spot on how to say things, how to word things. And so, I tend to ramble when I do get nervous, so I don't know if it would have changed anything.
>
> Q: Within the family?
>
> R: Within the family, yeah, it definitely would have changed me. It would have changed my views on it. It would have helped me change my views on it more, but I don't think that's just the type of person I am. A very private person. I don't want Lauren to feel that way. The Church of Christ is different now than it used to be. It's a lot more open. People are praying openly now. It's not so much that the men have to lead all of the prayers in the Bible classes. I want her to feel comfortable doing that when she's in the youth group.[18]

Attending Worship

Work and school are important, but not as important as spiritual matters. Mothers bring accountability to the spiritual part of life, and to attending worship in particular. One generation-one respondent recalls the influence of her mother:

---

[18] F19G3P1F, interview.

> I remember when I quit going to church there for a while when my children were young, my mother—when she found [out] about it—she said "Nancy, now you know what you're supposed to do." She didn't fuss at me or anything; she just said, well, you know.[19]

Her generation-two daughter recalls her consistent influence:

> My mother took the four of us to church alone. I'm sure, often didn't get anything out of the lessons, but she felt it was important for us to be at church. She lived it, she didn't just drag us to church; she tried to be what God wanted her to be.[20]

For some families, the church was the center of their social universe.

> Q: What are the most important things your parents did to help shape your faith?
>
> A: Live it. You know, they . . . we were talking last night, with the youth minister here, and one of the things that we pointed out was that our family, the center of everything, was God. Social, was God. And so, the center, the social center, geographic social center, of our lives was the church building. Because that's where God's people met and meet. What got us on to that was they've just moved to the area and are not living in town. They are living in a town ten miles away. And they were, we were talking about the positives and negatives of that, and their desire to get closer to the church building. Because that was going to be the center of their social existence. It wasn't going to be a school, it wasn't going to be a

[19] F11G1P1F, interview.
[20] F11G2P1F, interview.

> social organization, it was going to be God's people. And so, yeah. God. That was the center.[21]

In another family, a daughter recalls her mother's influence, even in the face of her father's indifference. "My mother was very strong even though my father didn't go to church, she always got us kids to church. So, I always really appreciated that."[22]

Living Moral Lives

Although many children and grandchildren remembered their matriarchs as Bible class teachers, others took up less public, yet important, roles in the church: "My mother wasn't as much a teacher, but she did things for those who were ill, for funerals and for the nursery in particular, she worked in it."[23] One generation-one respondent spoke of her mother's moral example in this way: "I think observing her life, her integrity, her honesty, always trying to do the right thing, serving other people, I think made a strong impression on me. I wanted to be like that. So, in her quiet way—not much verbal discussion with us about her faith—but it was more my observation of her demonstration of her faith."[24]

It should not be surprising that the voices of grandmothers speaking about their good works were often self-deprecating.

> Q: How do you see your role in your grandchildren's spiritual lives?
>
> A: I've thought of that actually . . . see myself like my grandmother because grandma wasn't overtly involved in anything but she was always there and supportive. I'm not the fun

[21] F3G2P1M, interview.
[22] F15G1P1F, interview.
[23] F22G1P1F, interview.
[24] F7G1P1F, interview.

> grandma that does stuff but I'm dependable. I'm the solid grandma; I'm just dependable.[25]

For other families, the moral lives of multiple generations were influential for family faith:

> They salted their speech with Godly talk. I remember hearing a lot, "the Lord willing." I heard "love," was a continuing word. In fact, my maternal grandmother had a phrase, "God love it." And that was kind of almost her Bible word, was "God love it." So yeah, it was their speech, it was . . . and they sought God's people. That was just their center. They decided to make that their center.[26]

Talking about Faith

As children begin to form their views of God, they may identify with the views of the same gender parent and grandparent; "I think I see God very similarly to the way my mother does. I think my dad being male probably has a little different look,"[27] observes a generation-two daughter about generation-one mother. Sometimes, though, offspring choose the view of the parent or grandparent that makes sense to them, not necessarily the view of the same-gender parent or grandparent. This generation-three son said,

> I think I have a closer relationship with God than my father does. But I think my mother and I have very similar views on God. The beauty of that similarity is that she never pushed that on me. Once I began to question some things, she

[25] F7G2P1F, interview.
[26] F3G2P1M, interview.
[27] F11G2P1F, interview.

> revealed similar sentiments, and we have good discussions about what God is like and what he desires from us.[28]

Notice that this son describes these faith conversations with his mother as ongoing: "We have good discussions." Here, a woman positively shapes the spirituality of her child and through her child, her grandchildren.

The voices of women can be especially significant in single-parent families. One generation-three daughter emphasizes this.

> Q: What are the most important things your parents did to help shape your faith?
>
> R: Since my dad was not in the picture [dad had divorced mom], Mom always taught me from an early age that it didn't matter that you didn't have an earthly father because you always have a heavenly Father. So, I think that being engraved into my mind at a young age has really shaped my spiritual beliefs today. And just her, mainly her persistence in making sure that I was always, you know, getting up and going to church, going to all the youth group activities, and keeping involved and wanting me to go to a Christian college. The conversations that we had together were always, everything was always centered around God.[29]

In conversations with these three-generation families, matriarchs—whether generation one, two, or three—had an abiding influence over the spiritual lives of their progeny. This is coherent with the work of other researchers who arrive at a similar conclusion.[30]

---

[28] F10G3P1M, interview.

[29] F25G3P1F, interview.

[30] Vern L. Bengtson, with Norella M. Putney and Susan Harris, *Families and Faith: How Religion Is Passed Down across Generations* (Oxford University Press, 2013), 116–17.

Legacy

We have talked about spiritual practices that empower grandmothers to walk alongside their offspring in lives of faith. These practices are important at the moment and yet they also shape the future. Who will we become? How will our children and grandchildren remember us? What will our legacy be? When we asked grandmothers about what they believed their legacy would be, they gave us a wide range of answers. Since grandparents tend to think about legacy quite a bit, it wasn't surprising that most of them had an answer; very few weren't sure or didn't know (see Figure 7.2)

The Legacy Grandmothers Are Leaving to Their Grandchildren

Legacy	Percent
Love God, love others	34.3
Good example	25.1
Be faithful	11.1
Jesus/God are most important	9.5
Not sure	5.0
Supporting family	4.6
Go to church	2.9
Trust God	1.9
Stick to the Bible	1.3
Sharing Christ	1.3
Servant	1.0
None	0.6
Do more spiritual things	0.4
Trust yourself/think for yourself	0.4
Prayer	0.4
Be accountable to God	0.2
Total	**100.0**

Figure 7.2

These answers prompt grandmothers to be intentional about what they hope their legacy to be. Who will they be and what will they do—day in and day out—to be seen as women of faith in the eyes of their grandchildren? Whatever practices grandmothers choose to pursue spiritually don't just shape their legacy for the grandchildren; they shape who they become. More about legacy in Chapter Eleven.

Implications

This chapter has brought many voices together in conversation to explore what it means to be a grandmother who walks alongside her children and grandchildren in faith. This work has shown that family members have identified prayer, Bible study, attending worship, living moral lives, and talking about faith as the central spiritual practices for faith families. The presence of parents and grandparents at mealtimes and bedtimes is particularly formative for children and frequently becomes the context for deeper questions and conversations. As rich and important as these intergenerational conversations are, a mother's and grandmother's offspring most often find themselves convicted of the importance of belief by "her demonstration of her faith."[31]

What importance does intergenerational faith have across three or more generations? Although some quantitative studies show that grandparents have a lesser effect on the faith of their grandchildren than the parents,[32] our quantitative grandparent study found that grandparents could be important in faith formation. When we asked grandparents about the most influential people in their faith, grandmothers were very important.

---

[31] F7G1P1F, interview.

[32] Christian Smith, with Melinda Lundquist Denton, *Soul Searching: The Religious and Spiritual Lives of American Teenagers* (Oxford University Press, 2005), 261.

- 31 percent much, most influential—maternal grandmothers
- 26 percent much, most influential—paternal grandmothers

These data show again that a line of grandmothers tends to have even more influence. The work of a first-generation grandparent in an intergenerational alliance with a second-generation parent may help that parent remain faithful. Such alliances have indirect but powerful consequences for the third generation.[33] Our study shows that a faithful matriarch or patriarch can be a stabilizing force during loss and stress for the resilience of families and the individuals within those families.[34] Multigenerational faith families do not necessarily have fewer trials. They are better equipped, though, to deal with them.

The ability of these families with a line of godly grandmothers to maintain a steady connection to a single faith group for several generations suggests that spiritual matriarchies are at least as, if not more effective in espousing healthy faith in the long term as patriarchies. Although matriarchs are as capable of abuses of power as patriarchs, especially as self-appointed gatekeepers of the faith, more often matriarchs prefer relational power over hierarchical. In our experience, these spiritual matriarchs usually exercise the power of connection, not compulsion.

---

[33] These "intergenerational alliances" can be helpful in healthy families and less so in families experiencing intragenerational conflict. Wesley R. Burr, Loren D. Marks, and Randal D. Day, *Sacred Matters: Religion and Spirituality in Families* (Routledge, 2012), 177–78.

[34] See Ron Bruner and Dudley Chancey, "Grief and Spiritual Coping: The Practices of Three Generations of Faith," *Discernment: Theology and the Practice of Ministry* 7, no. 1 (2021): 1–24, https://digitalcommons.acu.edu/discernment/vol7/iss1/1/.

Reflect and Discuss

1. What do you remember most about your grandmothers?
2. How did your grandmothers help you in your spiritual journey?
3. Discuss ways that your church empowers grandmothers to be grandmothers of faith.
4. Discuss the importance of being intentionally intergenerational in our families and our churches. How can each improve their practices and become even more intentional?
5. What are some specific practices that grandmothers can do to share their faith story with their grandchildren?
6. In our grandparent study and previous studies that are mentioned in this chapter, you will notice that *conversation* is important. In fact, the research shows that conversations about faith are more important in children's and grandchildren's faith development than even Bible reading, prayer, and attending church. What are some ways that grandmothers can be *more vocal* in sharing their faith story with their grandchildren?
7. Most of the participants in our study at one time or another chose "being a good example" as an answer to how they shared their faith. This is not all bad, but conversation is better. How do we move "being a good example" to vocally sharing our faith story? Discuss some ways those two can be tied together (e.g., being an example in serving others—take your grandchildren on a service project and tell them how serving others is your faith in action and a big part of your faith story so they see it and hear it).
8. Throughout this book, you have heard the importance of being present. How can grandmothers be more present in the lives of their grandchildren? How can grandmothers who are separated by distance be more present in the lives of their grandchildren?

9. What are some ways and ideas as to how grandmothers can create a living legacy with their grandchildren?
10. How can grandmothers be leaders in their friend circles, the community, and their churches?

CHAPTER EIGHT

The Importance of Grandfathers

It was a Friday in 2014. That day changed me from a father to a grandfather. I stood in the hospital that day holding my first grandchild. Over ten years have passed since then. Her family has grown, and we now have four granddaughters. In ten-plus years, I have learned much about being a grandfather. It is fun and exhausting.

Grandfathers can play a significant role in the life of their grandchildren. Can a child grow up without a grandfather? Yes. Will a child be better growing up with an intentional grandfather? Yes. Fathers (along with mothers) have the responsibility of protection, providing, and preserving and telling their children the great things God has done in their lives and in our world. In Bible times this telling the story of faith ran all the way up to the king (Deut. 17:18–19). Being a grandfather is one of my most important roles for the rest of my life. I think we did a fairly good job with our two boys growing up, and they are doing good jobs sharing their faith story with our grandchildren. We get to spend a good amount of time with our grandchildren because they live so close. We seize every opportunity to tell them the great things that God has done in our world—and that Jesus loves them.

As leaders of their families, fathers and grandfathers have many opportunities to see that their children know the great things that God has done in our world. In our world today, especially in North America, grandfathers are living longer, and some are directly involved in raising their grandchildren. Very early research on grandparents portrayed them in a negative light. Since the 1970s grandparents are shown to have more positive outcomes when dealing with their grandchildren. Grandfathers who are more religious tend to be more involved with their grandchildren. We see this most often when they are also connected to a community of faith. *Grandchildren notice their grandfathers in church settings.* When we asked college students about their grandfathers, we heard things like:

- He always took us to church.
- He was an elder in the church.
- He led singing till the day he died in our church—I can still hear his voice when we sing certain songs.
- He always led great prayers in our church.

The grandfathers portrayed above are the exception rather than the norm. Even in the Grandparent Project, 66 percent of the participants were female. It has been a challenge to convince grandfathers to participate. There were over three hundred grandfathers in the study, which provides a fair sample representing grandfathers. Be mindful that more involvement filling out a survey does not translate into more involvement of grandfathers telling their faith stories.

I am encouraged by the research coming out reporting on the importance of grandfathers' influence on grandchildren. In

2016 Olwyn Mark did an analysis of fifty-four published articles about the influence of grandparents.[1] He points out (as I continue to do in this book) that parents are the greatest influences on their children. This should be obvious, but it also highlights the importance of the grandparents. If they did their task properly with their children, and their children tell their faith story to their children, the grandchildren are in a win-win situation. Mark points out the highlights from the fifty-four studies that had reference to grandfathers:

- Foundations for faith are laid in childhood [start telling your faith story early].
- The role and responsibility of the family is central in faith transmission. . . .
- Enduring adolescent and adult believers are largely the product of caring, supportive, stable homes, where faith is seen, heard, and experienced.
- Modelling is key: parents [and grandparents] need to "be" and "do" what they want their child to become.

The remainder of this chapter will highlight specific things that were discovered in the Grandparent Project about grandfathers (and grandchildren).

Grandfathers Past and Present

In the past, grandfathers were stereotyped as strict, nonemotional, detached, and only present to provide harsh discipline as the keeper of the law. Most of this comes from books and movies where grandfathers are seen as very old, bent over, walking with a cane or in a wheelchair, or dying in a hospital bed. Grandfathers today are different. Many grandfathers are more educated, engaged

[1]Olwyn Mark, *Passing on Faith* (Theos, 2016), 12.

with their families, and excited to be able to make a difference in the lives of their grandchildren.

The grandfathers who took the Grandparent Project survey were well-educated (thirty-one terminal degrees, several master's degrees, and several MDs and DDs). While being educated and having good jobs would seem to be a plus, I also found it provides mobility and was the number one reason grandfathers gave for not being able to be with their grandchildren more—distance. They are in Florida, Arizona, or traveling to other places around the world. There is nothing wrong with this on the surface; it is a choice to be near or far for most of our grandparents.

In the Grandparent Project, 90 percent of the grandfathers grew up in a household with both parents present. Children raised in married parent homes are more likely to finish school and go to college. They are less likely to get in trouble, and they usually will have higher incomes and be married. Eighty-eight percent of the grandfathers are married. When they were asked how their relationship was with their adult children, 92 percent of the grandfathers said they had good relationships with their children (this alone is a big reason that they have access to their grandchildren). The relationship a grandparent has with their children affects their relationship with their grandchildren. Over 40 percent of the grandfathers agreed with that statement. I asked the grandfathers struggling with relationships with their children: What were some of the reasons for the struggle? Here is the list of the most given answers, with several very personal reasons not listed here:

- Bad feelings from the past that are not resolved (6 percent)
- Different political views (3 percent)
- Different views on raising children (5 percent)
- Changes in religious views (5 percent)

Divorce and marriage issues affected the faith of 12 percent of the grandfathers in the Grandparent Project study, which also affects the relationships they have with their grandchildren. Several grandfathers (13 percent) mentioned other family issues affecting their faith and their relationships.

Grandfathers Connecting

The grandfathers in the Grandparent Project would rather connect with grandchildren electronically versus writing cards and letters. They use texting, email, WhatsApp, Facebook, and other platforms that are introduced to them by their grandchildren. Who knew you could do Marco Polo without a swimming pool?

Matters of Faith and Legacy for Grandfathers

This Grandparent Project study all began as an investigation into how grandparents tell their faith story to the next generation. What do we have to do to not end up like much of Israel in the Old Testament? How do we go about telling the next generations the great things God has done in our world? I wanted to know how our participants learned about God and who told them the story. Parents are always the number one influence in children's lives, so do grandfathers matter in telling their grandchildren their faith story and the great things God has done and is doing in our world? Can they assist in helping their grandchildren grow spiritually?

Yes! Grandfathers can play a major part in the spiritual growth of their grandchildren. They can provide a family atmosphere for their children and grandchildren, they can be supportive, and they can model their faith. Grandfathers should also be speaking and teaching the importance of others telling their faith story in their churches and to other families. Young parents and parents-to-be need to hear these faith stories early on.

Over half of the grandfather participants in the Grandparent Project study are retired. While they may be retired from a career, they should not be retired from being one of the wise leaders of their family. The intergenerational messages that grandfathers can provide our families and our churches are invaluable. Research shows that quality of relationships, unity of traditions, and stability of the family structure provide the fertile soil for telling our faith stories.[2] Grandfathers who have "kept the faith" need to share their stories with their children and grandchildren, as well as other young people in their churches and communities. As children get older and begin to differentiate from their parents, grandfathers can be there as another voice affirming the continued faith formation journey that began with the parents. Teenagers learn from modeling. Seeing their dads and granddads "practice what they preach" is a very powerful way to tell the story. I asked grandfathers what they were doing to have a positive impact on their grandchildren's faith. The top five answers were:

- Love God, love others in front of them (87 percent)
- Reading the Bible in front of them and to them (45 percent)
- Praying in front of them and with them (79 percent)
- Going and taking them to church (71 percent)
- Being a good example in my marriage (82 percent)

Notice the first four of these (and probably the fifth) are done in the presence of the grandchildren. There is much to be said about *being present*. While many grandparents can't be physically present, I was recently reminded that one can be emotionally present. We also discuss ways to be in touch when you can't touch physically.

[2]Mark, *Passing on Faith*, 45.

Since telling the story is passed on from generation to generation (or not), I asked our grandfathers how they had come to faith and what difference hearing the story had made in their lives. I asked specifically about *their* grandparents. Which of their four grandparents was the most influential in their spiritual growth, and in what ways did that grandparent help them grow spiritually? Sadly, for our grandfathers many of them put "little," "no influence at all," and "negative influence" from their grandparents. There were several positive answers from the participants about the good influence from their grandparents. Notice that the most influential is female. We know from many studies that women tend to be more religious than men, and this certainly plays out here for the grandfathers in our sample. This is discussed more in other chapters.

- 31 percent much, most influential—mother's mother
- 22 percent much, most influential—mother's father
- 26 percent much, most influential—father's mother
- 16 percent much, most influential—father's father

Grandfathers were asked what the most influential grandparent did that helped them grow spiritually. Their answers ranged from reading the Bible to them (5 percent) and taking them to church (18 percent) to being a good example (32 percent).

Once again, these are about *being present*. There is a blog post from Legacy Coalition about being present and moving near your grandchildren.[3] I know that is not possible for everyone, but it really is something to think about if we want the next generations to know the great things that God has done in our world. I was speaking at a conference about grandparents, and a grandparent walked up to me afterward and told me that her daughter-in-law

[3]Gary Cardinal, "The Blessings of Presence," Legacy Coalition, February 5, 2024, https://www.legacycoalition.com/the-blessings-of-presence/.

was not taking her grandchildren to church. The grandparent told me they have decided to move to their son's city so they can take the grandchildren to church. *Being present* matters.

The grandfather participants were also asked about legacy. "Legacy" basically means something that is passed on. Things like money, property, faith, ethics, core values, and even your example. Your legacy could be a roadway for your grandchildren to follow. Your legacy should provide a rich heritage of inspiration for your family and even for your church and community. What will be said or written about you as a grandfather? The famous preacher Charles Spurgeon once said: "A good character is the best tombstone. Those who loved you and were helped by you will remember you when the forget-me-nots have withered. **Carve your name on hearts, not on marble**" (emphasis mine). I want my name carved on the hearts of my children and grandchildren.

I asked our grandfathers what legacy their grandparents left them. Some were sad and talked about how they did not receive any legacy from their grandparents (16 percent). Those who did receive a legacy mentioned the following:

- Loving God, loving others (10 percent)
- Being faithful to God and church (30 percent)
- Having close family ties (10 percent)
- Having a strong work ethic (9 percent)

I immediately asked our grandfathers what legacy they wanted to leave their grandchildren. One might think of legacy as investing. How we understand the concept of legacy largely will depend on what we think is most important. The previous list shows strong family and strong work ethic were just as important to our grandfathers as the greatest command (Matt. 22:37–39). The grandparents mentioned by our grandfathers grew up during the World Wars and the Great Depression and worked hard to survive and make a living for their family. I suspect that hard work and family got most of them through a very difficult time. The fact that being faithful to God and church (30 percent) was important to pass on speaks highly of a generation that many felt abandoned from the government and God. Many churches closed their doors for lack of funds. The grandfathers in the grandparent study gave the following answers as to what they wanted to leave behind as a spiritual legacy to their grandchildren:

- Loving God, loving others (27 percent)
- I want to be a good example to them (31 percent)
- Be a big supporting family (6 percent)
- I want them to know that Jesus and God are the most important (6 percent)
- I want them to be faithful to God and the church (19 percent)

The legacy they wanted to leave ran close to how they wanted to be remembered. I asked our grandfathers: Above all else, how would you like your grandchildren to remember you? When I think about children and being remembered, I am reminded of the adaptation of a quote from Forest Witcraft:

> One hundred years from now it will not matter what your bank account was, or the sort of house you lived in, or the kind of car you drove, but the world will be different because you were important in the life of a child.[4]

If you are a grandfather reading this chapter, put the names of your grandchildren in the place of "child." Seventy-seven percent of the grandfather participants said they believed they were important in the lives of their grandchildren. We are important in

---

[4]Forest Witcraft, "Within My Power," *Scouting* (October 1950).

their lives—we *should* be important in their lives. The grandfather participants in the Grandparent Project study said the following as to how they wanted to be remembered by their grandchildren:

- That I was faithful to God and church (34 percent)
- That I loved God and others (L1L2), especially my grandchildren (47 percent)
- That I was fun to be with (6 percent)
- That I was a servant (3 percent)
- That I was kind (3 percent)

Be reminded that this study was all about discovering how grandparents tell the story of their faith. I wanted to find out how, when, where, and why. At the very end of the survey, I asked our grandfathers, "What do successful grandfathers do to tell their faith story?" The following answers were given as to what the grandfathers heard from other grandfathers about being "successful in telling their faith story to their grandchildren":

- They shared their faith (8 percent)
- They were good Christian examples (52 percent)
- They spent time with grandchildren (25 percent)
- They were faithful to the church (12 percent)
- They were dedicated to their family (3 percent)

It was interesting to me that the word or concept of "sharing" did not come up until these last two questions. The idea of "sharing your faith" or "telling your faith story" seems foreign to our grandparents in general. (Hopefully by the end of this book, you will see why "telling your faith story" and "telling the great things that God has done and is doing in our world" will resonate with you.) However, the grandfather participants did use the term when they offered advice to grandparents who will be reading this book. I remember *Soul Searching* and the fact that the number one finding from that study of churched teenagers and their parents was that neither could tell their faith story—they could not "share" their faith.[5]

Faith stories resonate with people. I have found that when people hear my faith story and see how it fits into The Story, they begin to think about how maybe their story could fit into the bigger Story also. Learn to tell your faith story and tell your children and your grandchildren. How did you come to faith in Jesus? The grandfathers in the Grandparent Project study said the following is the advice they would give other grandfathers to help them tell their faith story to their grandchildren:

- Share your faith (13 percent)
- Pray and talk about faith (18 percent)
- L1L2—Love God, love others (15 percent)
- Take them to church (3 percent)
- Be faithful (5 percent)

This list screams out "modeling." Our children and grandchildren need to hear us tell our faith story and the great things God has done and is doing in our lives, but they also need to see us living it. Paul writes the following in Philippians 4:8–9 (emphasis mine):

> Finally, brothers and sisters, whatever is true, whatever is noble, whatever is right, whatever is pure, whatever is lovely, whatever is admirable—if anything is excellent or praiseworthy—think about such things. Whatever you have learned or received or heard from me, or seen in me—*put it into practice.* And the God of peace will be with you.

"Put it into practice." This is very bold of Paul to basically be saying that all the things he has been writing about in this letter,

[5]Christian Smith and Melina L. Denton, *Soul Searching: The Religious and Spiritual Lives of American Teenagers* (Oxford University Press, 2005).

he has done. He is saying, if you have seen me do it—you do it! Wow. Think about you and me as grandfathers. Can we look at our children and grandchildren and say, "Do what I do"? Is everything we do true, noble, right, pure, lovely, and admirable? I don't know about you, but I have a little work to do. I will say that having children and grandchildren makes you up your game. And whether we have children and grandchildren or not, we should all be doing what Paul talks about earlier in Philippians 3 when he says his goal is to *know* Christ. To be like him. If that is one of our first priorities, those adjectives in verse eight will come more naturally.

Cavin Harper in the book *Courageous Grandparenting* says grandfathers need to wake up, wise up, rise up, build up, and sign up to be intentional grandfathers.[6] He says the five things following here from the Christian Grandparenting Network can help us do that:

1. Keep in touch with his weekly newsletter.
2. Share the cause. Get other grandparents to be intentional.
3. Organize a grandfather small group in your neighborhood or church.
4. Participate in the national Grandparents' Day of Prayer each September.
5. Take seriously the discipling of the next generation to be faithful believers.

Challenges for Grandfathers

We live in a messed-up world. Until we meet Jesus or the world is made new, we must face each day intentionally living out the story and telling our faith story. Challenges will come up as they always have. Our children and grandchildren are watching us. They will

---

[6] Cavin Harper, *Courageous Grandparenting* (The Christian Grandparenting Network, 2013).

be able to tell if we really believe the story. If we really trust in God. Some believe that the four most important words in the Bible are in Genesis 1:1—"In the beginning God." When all else seems overwhelming, I think back to "In the beginning God" . . . and I trust that he will sustain us.

Older people face challenges almost daily with money issues, health issues, relationship issues, and caregiving issues, to name a few. I asked the participants in our study to discuss issues that were negatively affecting their faith and their ability to share their faith with their grandchildren. Divorce of the grandchildren's parents was a big deterrent in grandparents being able to connect with their grandchildren. Arber and Timonen devote a whole chapter in their book to the negative effects of divorce as it relates to grandparenting.[7] This shows up in the Grandparent Project as the largest item affecting grandfathers (27 percent). I have years of experience working in churches. I have witnessed the devastating results of divorce. The fighting and separation are terrible. Over 60 percent of grandparents who have married children have experienced at least one divorce.

This family breakdown influences grandfather identities. They begin as a grandfather. Divorce happens. If the grandfather is the paternal grandfather and his daughter-in-law gets custody of the grandchildren, there is a good chance that the "gatekeeper" will keep him out. He is out of a job (on the surface). In other cases, if the dad walks out on the family, there is a good chance that the grandfather may have to step into more of a father-type role. The dreams and thoughts of being that sweet ole grandpa who indulges his grandchildren can be shattered by divorce. New rules, new boundaries, new roles must be negotiated.

---

[7]Sara Arber and Virpi Timonen, eds., *Contemporary Grandparenting* (The Policy Press, 2012).

The second-highest issue affecting grandfathers in the study was a little surprising at first—church problems (23 percent). Almost one fourth of the grandfather participants chose this. Upon a closer look at the demographics of the grandparent study sample, I surmise that several of our grandfather participants probably hold or have held an office in the church (e.g., minister, elder, board member, committee member). The income, education, and careers of the men in our sample are demographics that fit many of our church leaders today. This is not to take away from the fact that some of our grandfathers are regular church members. Church splits and other church problems affect the whole church. In the churches I worked for, I was privileged to work beside some good grandfathers who were church leaders. They loved the church like they loved their grandchildren. I have had ministry friends who were not so lucky. The point here is that the relationships, the politics, and the usually unpaid work of church leaders takes its toll. If you are a grandfather in church leadership, I would highly suggest you read *Longevity in Leadership* by Lewis and Harrison.[8]

The third-highest issue in the grandparent study affecting the grandfathers' faith and their relationship with their grandchildren was conflict with their adult children—specifically children not attending church and not taking the grandchildren to church. I asked our participants if they gave their children the option to go or not go to church when they lived at home. Of the participants who did not make their kids go to church, 41 percent of those grandfathers say they are not satisfied with their children's church attendance now as adults. For the record, one-third (32 percent) of our grandfathers who made their children go to church were not satisfied with their children's current church attendance. It

[8] Phillip V. Lewis and John P. Harrison, *Longevity in Leadership* (Abilene Christian University Press, 2016).

should not be a surprise, as it has been noted in the research that if church is not important to parents, it will not be important to the children. You and I both know people who go to church just to check it off the weekly list. Children see through that. I have been asked by hurting grandparents: "How can I get my son or daughter to go to church and take our grandchildren?" Every case is different, and there is no one magic answer. If church and faith weren't a big deal to you when your children were growing up, you may need to do something big. Go to them and ask for forgiveness. Tell them you did not do a good job telling them the great things God has done and is doing in our world. Ask them for a chance to tell your faith story. Hopefully they have seen some changes in your life. Hopefully they will see the importance that you are placing on the spiritual side of life now. Don't expect overnight miracles. Well, maybe you should expect it, but don't be disappointed when it takes time.

As I go around the country presenting this study, it never fails that someone will tell me the story of their children not going to church and not taking the grandchildren to church. If you find yourself in this situation, stop reading this, and if needed, make a plan to go have a conversation with your children. Let them know now how important it is for you to tell your faith story and the great things God has done and is doing in our world. I have some great stories of grandparents packing up and moving to where their grandchildren live just to be able to take them to church, tell their faith story, and tell them the great things God has done and is doing in our world. ("Distance" was the number one answer that 43 percent of our grandfathers gave as to not being able to teach their grandchildren.)

The fourth-highest ranking issue for grandfathers was with same-sex attraction, LGBTQ, and transgender issues. While only 5 percent of grandmothers saw this as an issue, over 7 percent of grandfathers found this more troubling. This finding is consistent with current research which reports that females are more supportive of these issues than males.[9] A possible helpful article from *SilverSneakers* gives some advice to grandparents who have grandchildren who have "come out" (take the fish, leave the bones from articles like this one). The article mentions the following:

> A 2019 survey from AARP found that 88 percent of grandparents said they would accept a grandchild who came out to them as LGBTQ (lesbian, gay, bisexual, transgender, and queer or questioning). And that acceptance is very important for your grandchild's well-being. In a 2021 survey of nearly 35,000 LGBTQ youth, 62 percent reported symptoms of major depressive disorder, and 72 percent said they suffered from anxiety. Most worrisome of all, 42 percent said they'd considered suicide in the past year.[10]

The article gives grandfathers three tips to help navigate this growing issue: (1) listen with love (unconditional love), (2) deal with your own feelings, but not in front of your children and grandchildren, and (3) keep an open mind. Many children going through these changes are searching for that identity that we all went through. They need a wise, caring person they can talk with. One of the best pieces of advice I have heard around these issues for grandparents is to keep doing what you have been doing with your grandchild who is struggling. If you have been fishing together—keep fishing. If you have been golfing together—keep golfing. *Be present!*

---

[9] "Changing Attitudes on Same-Sex Marriage," Pew Research Center Fact Sheet, 2019, https://www.pewresearch.org/religion/fact-sheet/changing-attitudes-on-gay-marriage/.

[10] Nancy Fitzgerald, "How to Support Your LGBTQ Grandchild," *SilverSneakers* blog post, December 19, 2021, https://www.silversneakers.com/blog/how-to-support-your-lgbtq-grandchild/.

Mental and Physical Health

Aging brings on challenges with health and healthcare (see Chapter Five). I asked the study participants about mental and physical health issues that might keep them from being with their grandchildren. The participants in this Grandparent Project are mostly composed of baby boomers (born 1946 to 1964). While baby boomers are living longer, this generation has higher rates of obesity, diabetes, high cholesterol, and hypertension. Good news—the grandfathers in the study reported a slightly higher physical health report than our grandmothers. Seventy percent of our grandfathers reported that their health was high quality to very high quality. This gives baby boomers more opportunity to tell their faith story to their grandchildren.

Participants in the Grandparent Project were asked about an overall outlook on life. The questions asked were touching more on the side of their mental health status for the present and the future. The sixteen questions used for these measuring scales are in the footnotes for this chapter.[11] Research from Harvard University reports that people growing older who have a positive mental

---

[11] As I grow older, things seem better than I thought they would be.
I have gotten more of the breaks in life than most people I know.
I am just as happy as when I was younger.
These are the best years of my life.
I expect some interesting and pleasant things to happen to me in the future.
The things I do are as interesting to me as they ever were.
I feel old and somewhat tired.
I feel my age, but it does not bother me.
As I look back on my life, I am fairly well-satisfied.
I have made plans for things I'll be doing a month or a year from now.
I sometimes worry so much that I can't sleep.
I sometimes feel that life isn't worth living.
I am afraid of a lot of things.
Life is hard for me much of the time.
Most days I have plenty to do.
A person has to live for today and not worry about tomorrow.

outlook live longer and have fewer chronic illnesses.[12] Suggestions for grandfathers who struggle with a positive outlook included finding projects that match your values, teaching skills to others (78 percent of the grandfathers in our sample said they have shared skills with their grandchildren), stay away from the negatives, and stay socially active in your church and other organizations.

The sixteen questions collapsed into four items—Positive Outlook, Negative Outlook, Future Outlook, and Not Worried Outlook. Each participant received a score from 1–5 on each of the items (1=strongly agree to 5=strongly disagree). See Figure 8.1 below. The grandfathers score well on most of the items indicating a good outlook on life. The average scores (mean) are listed in the table. (Low scores on positive outlook, future outlook, and not worried outlook are better. High scores on negative outlook are better.) The grandfathers had better scores than the grandmothers.

a					
		Multi Item Scale (5 items) for Positive Outlook on Life	Multi Item Scale (4 items) for Negative Outlook on Life	Multi Item Scale (4 items) for Future Outlook on Life	Multi Item Scale (4 items) for Not Worried Outlook on Life
N	Valid	293	297	296	296
	Missing	35	31	32	32
Mean		2.3249	4.1279	2.0845	2.8395
a. What is your gender? = Male					

Figure 8.1

Our mental and physical health are important. The grandfathers in the Grandparent Project scored high in both areas. Many times, these factors determine whether a grandfather can spend

[12] "Positive Attitude about Aging Could Boost Health," Harvard T. H. Chan School of Public Health, last updated November 22, 2024, https://www.hsph.harvard.edu/news/positive-attitude-about-aging-could-boost-health/.

time with their grandchildren. Mentally healthier grandfathers are likely more involved and have higher levels of contact, commitment, and participation in activities.[13]

Remembering Grandfathers

Connected with the legacy questions in a later chapter was the question "How do you want to be remembered?" Two answers came to the top—"loving God and loving others" (38 percent) and "that I was faithful to God and church" (28 percent). The sad part of these questions was that sixty to eighty men did not answer certain ones of the three (some of them all three). I started fleshing that out in my Zoom and in-person interviews. When I would get to those questions and get no answer, I would probe a little deeper and ask why. I heard things like:

- "I'm not big on legacy."
- "Doesn't matter what I think, they will remember me how they want to—if they even do."
- "I don't think I have been around enough for them to even remember me."

I am convinced that many grandfathers do not realize the impact they can have on their grandchildren. If you are alive and they are alive, you still have time. Not surprisingly, there isn't that much spiritual advice here about sharing your faith story. From the Grandparent Project study and from the interviews completed, not many grandfathers have experience in "telling their faith story." One of the goals in putting this book together is to offer some help and resources for grandparents. This book provides ideas that will help all of us grandparents do a better job at the task of telling our

---

[13] James S. Bates and Alan C. Taylor, "Grandfather Involvement and Aging Men's Mental Health," *American Journal of Men's Health* 6, no. 3 (2012): 229–39.

faith story and the great things that God has done and is doing in our world to our grandchildren. *Grandfathers matter!*

Reflect and Discuss

1. What can be done to make some grandfathers realize they can be important in the lives of their grandchildren?
2. Would grandfathers attend a grandfather support group specifically about spiritual life?
3. What would be a good format for that support group?
4. What does or could your church do to empower grandfathers?
5. As a grandfather, what skills do you have that you could teach your grandchildren?
6. What could you teach your sons and grandsons about how to take care of your spouse?
7. What things are you doing to maintain your health that you could share with your group?
8. What advice would you give new grandfathers?
9. What has been the greatest challenge for you as a grandfather with your grandchildren?
10. If you are the grandfather of only granddaughters, what have been the challenges for you to connect with the girls?

CHAPTER NINE

How Grandparents Share Their Faith Story

Not much has been reported in the United States about faith transmission. This chapter will look at the results of the grandparent study as participants were asked how faith was transmitted to them; how they are transmitting faith to their children and grandchildren; and how they have seen their peers transmit faith successfully.

This chapter will give insight into what I feel is the most important task of people who believe in God—telling the world about the great things he has done and is doing in our world. We do this in a powerful way by telling our faith story—specifically how God has been involved in our lives. Even though parents are the most important people in the lives of their children, we know as grandparents that we can play a part, especially as we support our adult children as they raise our grandchildren. This is key! Keep in mind as you read this chapter that you will see mention of "passing on faith" or "transmitting faith" in studies that have been done. I have chosen "sharing your faith story" as the language to replace "passing" and "transmitting" language.

The intergenerational transmission of religion is associated with better family functioning and relationships.[1] One of the reasons Oklahoma Christian's Intergenerational Faith Center was created was to study why children were dropping out of our churches and how that was affecting families and churches. The United States has become a mission field, currently hosting more than thirty-two thousand missionaries from other countries.[2] This is largely due to aging churches in the United States and the US hosting many displaced people from around the world. This is not all doom and gloom bad news. While many churches are "turning gray," many new churches are springing up. Early research by Barna reported the growth of the house church movement in this country. In 2006 the growth rate was up 9 percent, and it was projected to continue to grow.[3] Many of our millennial and Gen Z children are not dumping Jesus and church, they are just doing it differently.

The Grandparent Project study participants were asked several questions about spiritual and faith matters pertaining to their grandchildren. In the next few pages, look at the items and see where you stand compared to the study participants. For example, when participants were asked to discuss sharing their faith across the generations, I wanted to know about their grandparents. Did those grandparents share their faith with our participant grandparents? Figure 9.1 gives us an idea of who was spiritually

[1]Heather H. Kelley, Quinn Galbraith, and Byran B. Korth, "The How and What of Modern Religious Transmission and Its Implications for Families," *Journal of Family Psychology* 35, no. 4 (2021): 423–32.

[2]Cris Alley, "How Far Are Missionaries Sent?," Union Baptist Association, https://www.ubahouston.org/blog/missionary-sending-cohort-diaspora.

[3]Barna Group, "House Church Involvement Is Growing," Barna, June 19, 2006, https://www.barna.com/research/house-church-involvement-is-growing/.

influential in the lives of our participant grandparents when they were young.

Type of Influence	Mother's Mother	Mother's Father	Father's Mother	Father's Father
Negative Influence	1%	4%	3%	4%
No Influence	25%	37%	30%	43%
Some Influence	26%	23%	27%	22%
Much Influence	23%	16%	18%	13%
The Most Influence	14%	7%	9%	3%

Figure 9.1

Looks like maternal grandmothers win again with 23 percent "much influence" to 14 percent being the "most influential" in the participant grandparents' lives (out of 995 participants). These results show that the older generation weren't exactly the spiritual giants in their time as far as sharing their faith story and the great things God has done and is doing in our world. Keep in mind that the Barna study on aging well pointed out that this older generation saw their religion as being very private.[4] This could be the reason for the low numbers. There were two world wars and the Depression going on in their lifetimes. You might think that people would be more religious during those times.

I did my dissertation at the University of Tennessee, Knoxville, in the early 90s. At that time several large employers in the area were having cutbacks and layoffs. We did a random phone survey to see how the economic distress in the area was affecting people.[5] My part of the survey was developing questions about religiosity and faith. I wanted to know if people's faith and religion increased,

---

[4]Matthew Leighty, *Aging Well: A Renewed Vision for Ministering to Older Adults* (Barna, 2023).

[5]Greer Litton Fox and Dudley Chancey, "Sources of Economic Distress: Individual and Family Outcomes," *Journal of Family Issues* 19, no. 6 (1998): 725–49.

decreased, or stayed the same during stressful times. It might seem logical to think that people's faith increases during difficult times. This was not the case. In that survey, a very small group of single-parent mothers said that their faith had increased. Overall, religiosity by itself was not a predictor of self-satisfaction in that study. We also know that high education levels and high incomes can be a factor in the limited use of religiosity. As I look at the Grandparent Project, the grandparents are very educated and have high incomes overall. (Keep these two things in mind as we think about why the grandparents in the Grandparent Project might not be active in telling their faith story.)

A follow-up question was asked about the most influential grandparent in the Grandparent Project: "How did that most influential grandparent help you grow spiritually?" Notice in Figure 9.2 that only 7 percent of these grandparents shared their faith. The list below has some great attributes, but there is not much "telling." Most likely the parents of the participant grandparents in the study got the same treatment—attend church, be a good person. Keep this in mind when looking at what the grandparents in the Grandparent Project are doing for their grandchildren spiritually.

How Grandparents Helped You Grow Spiritually	
Attend Church Together	30%
By Their Example	40%
Christian Influence / Shared faith	7%
Unconditional Love	6%
Taught Me the Bible	2%
Devotion to Family	1%
Read Bible / Prayed with Me	9%
Singing	1%
Paid for Christian College	1%
Loved Us	1%
Taught Us Skills	1%
Bought My Church Clothes	1%

Figure 9.2

I will continue to mention Psalm 71 and 78 throughout this book. The urgency to share our faith stories with our grandchildren has never been greater. Near the end of the Grandparent Project survey, grandparents in the study were asked, "What do you understand your biblical duty to be in passing the faith to your children and grandchildren?" Only 2 percent of our participants said, "It is the parents' job to pass on faith, not the grandparents.'" Ninety-four percent of the participants chose "Every adult has the responsibility to pass on the faith to the following generations." I think the 94 percent is on to the right answer, but there is more. When you look back to Chapter Four about styles and roles of grandparents, you may not see grandparents as disciple-makers. They should be. The D6 Family gives some insight into why grandparents of today may not see their role as disciple-makers clearly in Scripture.[6] (The word "grandparent" started appearing in the 1800s.) The Bible speaks of roles for husbands, wives, and children. A closer look at Scripture points out the important role of grandparents:

- "Teach [God's commands] to your children and to their children after them" (Deut. 4:9).
- "Fear the LORD your God, you and your son and your son's son, by keeping all his statutes and his commandments, which I command you, all the days of your life, and that your days may be long" (Deut. 6:2 ESV).
- "Tell to the coming generation the glorious deeds of the LORD . . . which he commanded our fathers to teach to their children, that the next generation might know them, the children yet unborn" (Psalm 78:4–6 ESV).

---

[6]"Understanding the Biblical Role of Grandparents," D6 Family Ministry, https://d6family.com/understanding-the-biblical-role-of-grandparents/.

These verses may help you to see the importance of grandparents sharing their faith story and telling the great things that God has done and is doing in our world. If you need it clearer, here is my own paraphrase of the three verses:

- "**Grandparents** teach God's commands to your children and your **grandchildren**" (Deut. 4:9).
- "Fear the LORD your God, **grandparents** and your children and your **grandchildren**, by keeping all his statutes and his commandments, which I command you, all the days of your life, and that your days may be long." (Deut. 6:2).
- "Tell the coming generation the glorious deeds of the LORD . . . which he commanded our **grandparents** to teach to their children, that the next generation might know them, the **grandchildren** unborn" (Psalm 78:4–6).

At this point I know that some of you are hurting because some of your children may have walked away from faith and church. Some may not even let you speak of faith and church to their children, your grandchildren. How do you share your faith story in those situations?

Two sets of grandparents shared their struggles with me. One set only gets to see their grandchildren once a year. They expressed to me that those few hours were the best time of the year for them. They were upbeat and positive even though they could not speak of the most important thing in life to them; they showed unconditional love to their grandchildren and to their unbelieving children. Another couple shared that they could only see their grandchildren once a year at Christmas. They also said that was the most important week of the year for them. They were able to share their faith stories with their grandchildren during this time. Both sets took full advantage of the allowed time. They did not spend it trying to undermine the parents or be negative. Family unity and warmth are a big deal.

Tips for Grandparents with Nonbelieving Children

- Project God's character through your winsome attitude and lifestyle.
- Respect your nonbelieving children by promoting family unity.
- Spend time with your grandkids [within the boundaries set by parents].
- Invite the grandkids to go to church with you [if the parents allow].
- Concretely demonstrate your spiritual life and relationship with God.
- Talk about God's work in your life [this is sharing your faith story].
- Communicate everyday biblical principles without preaching.
- Reinforce the importance of righteousness in every area of life.
- Watch for signs of spiritual readiness.
- Demonstrate the love of God through carefully chosen gifts.
- Offer interesting books that pique spiritual interest.
- Endure scoffing with grace.
- Love and encourage your nonbelieving children.[7]

[7] Annie Yorty, "How to Share the Gospel with Your Grandkids If the Parents are Non-Believers," Crosswalk, last updated February 6, 2025, https://www.crosswalk.com/family/parenting/grandparenting/how-to-share-the-gospel-with-your-grandkids-if-the-parents-are-non-believers.html.

The grandparent participants in the Grandparent Project were asked, "What are you currently doing to have a positive impact on your grandchildren's faith?" Figure 9.3 shows the most chosen answers. Participants could choose as many as applied to them.

Impact on Grandchildren	
Loving God and loving others in front of my grandchildren	87%
Reading the Bible in front of them and to them	49%
Praying in front of them and with them	76%
Going to church and taking them to church	72%
Being a good example in my marriage	73%

Figure 9.3

A little over 14 percent of the participants had other things that they felt were making a positive impact on their grandchildren. These are listed in Figure 9.4.

Impact on Grandchildren (Other)	Participants	
Praying for them	8	6%
Encouraging them to be faithful	12	9%
Being a good example to them	19	14%
Talking about God's creation	2	1%
Being present	18	13%
Talking with them about God	25	18%
Singing Christian songs	6	4%
Showing them how to care for others	7	5%
Going with them on mission trips and camps	6	4%
Giving Bibles / Teaching them the Bible	28	20%
Paying for Christian school / camps	4	3%
Church	5	4%

Figure 9.4

I do want to point out that these are good and positive things to do with grandchildren. I also want to keep pushing that we must tell—tell our faith story and the great things God has done and is doing in the world.

Then the grandparent participants in the Grandparent Project were asked, "Did you have any expectations for your parents to pass on their faith to your children (their grandchildren)?" Over half (61 percent) said "yes" and 30 percent said "no." A follow-up question was asked, "If your children knew your parents, what ways did you see your parents intentionally passing on their faith to your children?" This was exciting, in that one-third (32 percent) of the grandparents said their parents shared their faith story with their children (Figure 9.5).

Your parents intentionally passing faith to your children	
Reading the Bible to them	29%
Praying with them	46%
Sharing their faith story with them	32%
Taking them to Sunday school and church	45%
Teaching them life lessons based on their faith	45%
Being examples on how to treat people	75%
Telling them constantly that Jesus loves them	30%

Figure 9.5

I followed up these questions by asking the study participants if they knew any other grandparents who were successfully passing on their faith to their grandchildren, and if so, what were some of the things they were doing (Figure 9.6)? Only two-thirds of our participants knew someone.

Successful grandparents passing on faith	
Share their faith	9%
Be good Christian examples	51%
Spend time with grandchildren	22%
Be faithful and dedicated to God and Church	16%
Be dedicated to family	2%

Figure 9.6
(37 percent of our participants did not answer this question.)

I have used the word "successful" a few times. There are many aspects to being a successful grandparent, and many of those are probably subjective at best. The authors of *Families and Faith* explored how faith is passed down across generations.[8] Several articles have been written from their study of families. The most salient finding from the book is the idea of "warmth." None of the things in this chapter about how we do or do not tell our faith stories matter if we do not have quality relationships with our adult children and grandchildren—emotional bonding.

In addition, the article mentions some best practices for grandparents who want to share their faith. These include prayer, telling family stories, modeling faith, sharing unhurried time, and spoiling and blessing them.[9] Many of you reading this will have opportunities to be with your grandchildren. Use the time wisely. Here are three ways to use your time with your grandchildren:

1. Tell your faith story. Tell how you came to faith in Christ. (There is some good advice in this article on how to share your faith story.[10])
2. Tell them about times when you had doubts and how God got you through those times.
3. Tell them about times where God proved his faithfulness to you and how he is your past, present, and future hope.[11]

---

[8] Vern Bengtson, with Morella M. Putney and Susan Harris, *Families and Faith: How Religion Is Passed Down across Generations* (Oxford University Press, 2013).

[9] Holly C. Allen and Heidi S. Oschwald, "The Spiritual Influence of Grandparents," *Christian Education Journal* 5, no. 2 (2008).

[10] Sherry Schumann, "How to Share Your Faith Story with Your Grandchildren," *Sherry Schumann* blog, October 26, 2020, https://sherryschumann.com/how-to-share-your-faith-story-with-your -grandchildren/.

[11] "Grandparents: Share Your Faith Story," Empowered Homes, https://empoweredhomes.org/resource/grandparents-share-your-faith-story/.

Sharing Your Faith Long-Distance

For those of you who are long-distance grandparents, you still must share your faith story. Other chapters in this book talk about the different ways grandparents in the Grandparent Project stay in touch with their grandchildren. Be intentional!

Wayne Rice was the co-founder of the largest youth ministry conference in the world: Youth Specialties. I attended that conference for over twenty years. Wayne transitioned into doing senior ministry (at the Legacy Coalition) in the last few years and does writing and speaking about grandparenting. He wrote a book especially for long-distance grandparents titled *Long-Distance Grandparenting.*[12] Here are some quick tips he gives (used with permission) on staying connected:

Plaster Your Home with Photos and Reminders of Your Grandchildren

After all, that's what refrigerator doors are for! Ask your grandchildren (or their parents) to provide you with updated school and family photos as well as their artwork and other visual reminders of your grandchildren so that you can display them all over your home. If you see your grandchildren every day (even in pictures), you will be more likely to do this next step.

Pray Daily for Your Grandkids

The most important and reliable connection between you and your long-distance grandchildren is prayer. Even though you are far away from your grandchildren, prayer can bring you and your grandkids together in a significant and powerful way. With God, there is no distance at all between you and your grandkids. Ask your grandchildren for prayer requests and let them know that you are praying for them. They may also want to pray for you.

---

[12] Wayne Rice, *Long-Distance Grandparenting: Nurturing the Faith of Your Grandchildren When You Can't Be There in Person* (Bethany House Publishers, 2019).

Put the Grandkids on Your Calendar

Don't let poor planning keep you away from your grandchildren. Life can get busy. If you don't plan to do something, it will likely not get done. So why not create a calendar especially with your grandchildren in mind? When can you visit them? When can they visit you? What about phone or video calls? Will you do these on a weekly, biweekly, or monthly basis? Do you have your grandchildren's birthdays and other special days on your calendar? A little planning can go a long way toward bridging the long-distance gap with your grandkids.

Put the Grandkids in Your Budget

You can pretty much take it to the bank that the farther away your grandchildren live from you, the more expensive it will be for you to stay connected, especially if travel is involved. What you don't want to do is give your grandkids the leftovers of your budget (you won't have anything left).

Plan Regular Visits

Or consider taking the grandchildren with you as you travel. Work with your grandchildren's parents to visit at a convenient time and share expenses. Make your visits memorable, and your grandchildren will always look forward to them.

Arrange for Them to Visit You

Sometimes it's easier to bring the grandchildren to you than it is to visit them. Find out when the grandchildren have time off from school and other activities and make travel arrangements. Some long-distance grandparents plan annual "cousin camps" when all the grandkids come to grandma and grandpa's house for a week of fun and family time.[13]

[13]Susan Alexander Yates, "A Band of Cousins—Encouraging Family Bonding," Focus on the Family, July 2020, https://www.focusonthefamily.com/parenting/a-band-of-cousins/.

Use Snail Mail

Also known as the US Postal Service, snail mail may be relatively slow, but it's still something that we can use very effectively to stay in touch with our grandkids. Everyone loves to get something personal in the mail, and grandkids are no exception. Send letters, postcards, gifts, money, anything that can be mailed. A weekly postcard from grandma or grandpa is an inexpensive and effective way to stay in touch. Get creative and let your grandkids know what's going on in your life in twenty-five words or less. They will love it and look forward to each one.

Use the Telephone

Most of today's children have (or at least have access to) a phone that they can use to stay in touch with family and friends. So, make a habit of calling your grandkids regularly. If you can, call each grandchild separately so that they get your special attention. Keep a notebook and write down things you hear them say so that you can follow up the next time you call. You can pray for them on the phone and offer your blessing for them as well.

Send Text Messages

While we're on the subject of phones, most kids love to send and receive text messages. Short text messages let your grandchildren know that you are thinking about them and are willing to share your life with them as well.

Video Chat Your Grandkids

Today's technology makes it possible for you to have face-to-face conversations with your grandchildren on your computer, tablet, smart TV, or cell phone. Applications like Zoom and FaceTime are useful at this writing. Always ask your grandchildren how best to connect electronically with them. Email still works. If you are not familiar with using them, have someone else help you get a simple setup so that you can take advantage of this truly wonderful way to connect with your grandchildren.

These are just a few good ways to reduce the distance between yourself and your grandchildren; but remember, none of them happen automatically. They require that we catch the vision for biblical, intentional grandparenting and put them into practice regularly. It is possible to share God's love with your grandchildren, no matter how far away they may be. If you have friends who are attempting to share their faith story with their children and grandchildren, but they give excuses as to why they can't do it, tell them to check out the Dare 2 Share website. It has helps and resources and a list of excuses people give to not share their faith.

Some Final Thoughts

Telling our faith story is important. We know that most of you reading this book would agree. Unfortunately, we are not getting it done. It is all about relationships first. In the Grandparent Project, 91 percent of the participants said they had a good relationship with their children. When spouses are added to that question, the percentage only drops by 3 to 88 percent. When we throw grandchildren into the mix, the numbers drop to half.

I asked whether the relationship with their children affects the relationship with their grandchildren. The responses were "some" 22 percent and "a lot" 41 percent. It appears on the surface that the grandparents in the Grandparent Project believe they have a good relationship with their adult children, but looking deeper, the relationships may not be that good. We know that money, divorce, politics, and religion can upset relationships in families. In the grandparent study, 42 percent of our participants said that life events in their families had created problems with their faith or religion. For example, some mentioned how their children stopped attending the church where they grew up. They changed church affiliations and took their children with them. This caused division in several of our participants' families. Faith, religion, and church became topics that were off limits when families got together. A few participants mentioned that they do not talk to their children or grandchildren because they have "left the faith."

Back to our "warmth" concept. It is all about relationships first. The authors of *Handing Down the Faith* report findings from previous research about the importance of relationships and faith.[14] They say warm, affirming relations are vital, including:

- Quality conversations
- Children-centered religious conversations—not adult-centered
- Fathers filling their role—being there
- Parents sharing the same faith tradition
- Two-parent households
- Grandparents who substitute, reinforce, moderate
- Too much or too little is not good—be intentional, consistent, and actively engaged
- Don't be a hypocrite
- Children influence parents also (reciprocal relations)
- Parents' effects on children's religion also have effects on other parts of their lives

If you are having trouble sharing your faith story with your grandchildren, it may not be because of relationship problems. Make sure you are leading out in family unity. It is all about relationships first. In a recent book titled *Religious Parenting*, the

[14] Christian Smith and Amy Adamczyk, *Handing Down the Faith: How Parents Pass Their Religion on to the Next Generation* (Oxford University Press, 2021), 4–6.

authors propose a finding in their research called "family solidarity."[15] They share the following from their research:

> The Importance of Family Solidarity: Parents desire to have warm, close relationships with and among their grown children in the future (harmony while children live at home is not necessarily to be expected). Major differences or divisive conflict with or alienation from or between adult children would be deeply saddening. Anything parents can do in the present to foster a family cohesion that will continue into the empty-nest decades—such as fostering common recreational interests like sports, political views, and basic life values—is therefore important, including working to pass on the family religion. Families that agree on the same religious beliefs, practices, and ways of talking enjoy a particularly strong basis of harmony and cohesion, because shared religion is a potent source of family solidarity. In some cases, family solidarity can even be stronger than religion.

Who better to challenge us here than our grandchildren? I asked college students, "What do you think would be the most important things for grandparents to pass on to their grandchildren? What do you think they should be teaching you as their grandchild?" Here are some of the answers they gave us, not in any order of significance, in Figure 9.7. You may not have a clue about some of these, but the beauty is that you say, "Let's find out together." These are faith issues. You probably could answer several of these just by telling your faith story. Show your grandchildren this list and see what they might choose to talk about.

---

[15] Christian Smith, Bridget Ritz, and Michael Rotolo, *Religious Parenting: Transmitting Faith and Values in Contemporary America* (Princeton University Press, 2020), 142–43.

Acceptance	Are we all equal in God's eyes?	Be accountable to others
Be salt and light	Bible is absolute truth	Care for others
Christ's love for the downtrodden	Community	Compassion
Desire to know the truth	Discipline	Don't conform to the world
Evangelism	Forgiveness of sins	Fruits of the Spirit
God and Jesus love you	God is holy	God's unconditional love
The Golden Rule	The gospel: creation, fall, redemption	Great Commission
Guard against temptation	Honesty	Hope
How to build relationship with God	How to live your life for God	How to love God and creation
How to study the Bible	Humility	Importance of church community
Importance of God's Word	Importance of faith	The Incarnation
Jesus died for us to save us	Jesus will return	Jesus's birth, death, resurrection
John 3:16	Justice and mercy	Keep the Word in your heart
Kindness	Let people see Christ in you	Listen to others
Live your life for God and Jesus	Love God, love others	Worship God, no others
Nothing can separate you from God	Obedience/morals	Patience
Personal relationship with Christ	Pray all the time	Put others first
Relying on God's daily guidance	Repentance	Respect all and yourself
Responsibility	Sacrificial living	Salvation through Jesus
Saved by grace	Sermon on the Mount	Serve others
The Ten Commandments	Trust that God is in control	We sin, but Jesus saves us
What are the idols in our lives today?	What does give generously mean?	You can have questions about God

Figure 9.7

You can do this!

In the end, you must figure out how best to share your faith story. Do this important task while respecting the boundaries set up by your adult children. "Go tell it on the mountain," but tell it at home first!

For those of you who like resources that are simple and easy to use, check out the Appendix. There is a lesson there from a dissertation by Leon Sanderson from Memphis, Tennessee (used with permission). He did this project for the church where he was working. He wanted the leadership to see the importance of the senior members of the church, to provide lessons that these senior members could use in reaching out to their grandchildren and other children in the church. The lesson in the Appendix is about sharing your faith story. You can also find other resources from the Grandparent Project on the Intergenerational Faith Center's website. Check out "The Spiritual Journey of Grandparents" and "What Successful Grandparents Do."[16]

Reflect and Discuss

1. Did you ever take an evangelism class at your church growing up? If "yes," describe it and tell what methods were taught.
2. Have you ever studied the Bible with someone who was not a believer? If "yes," talk about the experience.
3. Do you have a method that you use to share your faith with others?
4. Which of the topics in the list in Figure 9.7 do you feel comfortable or knowledgeable about to discuss with others?
5. Which of the topics in the list do you not have a clue about?
6. Do you have friends you hang out with who are not believers?

---

[16] The Grandparent Project, "The Spiritual Journey of Grandparents" and "What Successful Grandparents Do," Intergenerational Faith Center website, https://www.oc.edu/intergenerational-faith-center/ifc-resources.

7. Does the church you attend have an outreach program for evangelism? What methods are they using?
8. What could your church do right now to help you in reaching your friends with the gospel?
9. Which of the excuses from the Dare 2 Share website have you used?
10. Ask this question to yourself. "If the Bible is true, what should I be doing?"

CHAPTER TEN

A Few Words from Grandchildren

When grandchildren are asked what they want to know about or from their grandparents, research shows they want to hear stories about when their grandparents were young. Some grandchildren want to know where their grandparents came from and what their heritage is. Many grandchildren want to hear advice and wisdom from their grandparents. These different avenues of communication provide us opportunities to share our faith story and tell about the great things God has done and is doing in our world.

If you are blessed to live and watch your grandchildren grow to be adults, you may be reminded of the stages of development that their parents (your adult children) went through as you raised them. The key here is to know that the grandchildren are developing, and their attitudes and behavior toward you will change. In 1970, one study explored the meaning of being grandparents from the grandchildren's perspective.[1] The study found that four- and five-year-olds valued grandparents for the indulgent qualities. The eight- to nine-year-olds reported that they loved all the fun activities they did with their grandparents. The older group in the study (eleven- to twelve-year-olds) began showing distancing from the grandparents. When eighteen- to twenty-six-year-old grandchildren were asked about their relationships with their grandparents, they reported that they did not see their grandparents as old-fashioned or out of touch, that they were a big influence on them, and that they felt a responsibility toward their grandparents.[2]

In most of the studies I looked at for information and resources, closeness and proximity surfaced in every study. Over and over grandchildren would report closeness as the number one reason for their good relationship with their grandparents. *Being present matters.* In 1992 a sample of grandchildren in college was asked, "What makes a successful relationship with you and your grandparents?"[3] Five qualities surfaced in this study:

- A fairly high degree of closeness
- A strong sense of being known by the grandparents
- A strong sense of the young adult's knowing the grandparents
- A sense of the grandparent being a fairly strong influence in the life of the grandchild
- A sense of an authentic or independent grandparent/grandchild relationship not dominated by, but supported by, the middle generation

---

[1] Boaz Kahan and Eva Kahana, "Grandparenthood from the Perspective of the Developing Grandchild," *Developmental Psychology* 3, no. 1 (1970): 98–105.

[2] Joan F. Robertson, "Significance of Grandparents: Perceptions of Young Adult Grandchildren," *The Gerontologist* 16 (1976): 137–40.

[3] Gregory E. Kennedy, "Quality in Grandparent/Grandchild Relationships," *The International Journal of Aging and Development* 35, no. 2 (1992): 83–98.

In all these studies, keep in mind that your grandchildren are growing up and going through changes. Those changes are happening even faster than we can keep up with. This makes it even more important for you to tell your faith story and all the great things that God has done and is doing in our world—early and often.

One of my favorite grandparent studies asked grandchildren to draw pictures of their grandparents.[4] When authors reviewed the drawings and compared them to the ways the grandchildren related to their grandparents, three areas surfaced from the drawings (these are included in the appendix of their book):

> Group 1—Children who have close contact with their grandparents portray them as large, active, fully viewed figures dominating the page, indicating their intimate knowledge of them.
>
> Group 2—Children who have sporadic contact with their grandparents tend to draw them in a variety of ways that indicate a lack of intimate knowledge of them. Themes of abandonment and detachment predominate (i.e., scenes of leave takings are commonly drawn).
>
> Group 3—Children who have minimum or no contact with their grandparents draw distorted, bizarre, and unrealistic images drawn primarily from their imaginations. They do not draw real people, indicating they have no knowledge at all of a real grandparent—it's like taking a test in a subject never studied.

How would your grandchildren draw you? I have a book in my library titled *My Favorite Book*. It is my favorite book because it has all the drawings my two sons did for me growing up (stopped

---

[4] Arthur Kornhaber and Kenneth L. Woodward, *Grandparents/Grandchildren: The Vital Connection* (Routledge, 1985), Appendix.

at the teenage years—it wasn't cool anymore). Most of them are birthday cards that they made by hand. Almost all of them are about things we did together—golf, sailing, working. It is priceless. Vicki does crafts with our four granddaughters. They love to draw pictures and paint on canvas. It is always about us being together. *Being present* matters.

Refer back to Figure 9.7 in Chapter Nine. I believe it makes a point about the importance of grandchildren's voices. For the grandparent study, I asked college students, "What do you think would be the most important things for grandparents to pass on to their grandchildren? What do you think they should be teaching you as their grandchild?" The answers provided in Figure 9.7 give grandparents many things to talk about. Find out which ones resonate with each grandchild and go for it.

Most of the topics in the list are faith issues. You probably could talk about several of these just by telling your faith story and the great things God has done and is doing in our world today. Show your grandchildren this list and see what they might choose to talk about. They may have more topics to add. Listen.

Story in the Bible about Faith Sharing

I asked college students (grandchildren) to tell me about a story in the Bible where parents, grandparents, or elderly people shared their faith story. One interesting finding with this question was that only fifty of the eighty-nine students had an answer for it. Thirty-nine students left this blank. These were honors students at a Christian university. As you look at this list, many of these stories the other fifty students mentioned are about the great things God did in history. Some may be a stretch for how effective the storyteller was, but at least they thought they knew a story. (Several of the students named the same story.)

Proverbs—train up a child
Deuteronomy
Paul's letters
Eunice, Lois, and Timothy
The Exodus
Thomas in the New Testament
Moses leading Israel
Ephesians
Psalm 100
Abraham to Isaac
Psalm 78
Isaiah 40:30–31
Jesus talking to children
Samuel
Nation of Israel
David and Solomon
Naomi to Ruth
Isaac to his children
Titus 2—older teach younger
Paul to Timothy
Moses and Joshua
Noah and his family

Below are some conclusions from a 2016 study by Barna Research about students and the Bible:

1. Reading the Bible in public is seen as encouraging
2. A majority of teens own a Bible and read it regularly
3. A majority of teens read the Bible for more than fifteen minutes each sitting
4. Growing closer to God is the key motivator for Bible reading
5. Teens still prefer to use a hard copy Bible in a digital age
6. The Bible is considered sacred literature
7. The Bible is a source of hope and guidance
8. The Bible is considered the literal or inspired Word of God
9. The Bible should have more influence on society
10. The Bible influences political decisions[5]

At the time of this 2016 study by Barna, David Kinnaman, the president of Barna Group, had this to say:

> In an increasingly secular culture, the Bible remains a highly regarded and well-read text among the vast majority of

---

[5]Barna Research, "Top 10 Findings on Teens and the Bible," Barna, August 26, 2016, https://www.barna.com/research/top-10-findings-teens-bible/.

> American teens—most of whom believe it to be sacred. And the fact that so many still consider it a source of hope and guidance is reason for great optimism for church leaders and parents alike.
>
> The explosive growth of digital technology and mobile devices presents a unique opportunity for Bible engagement among the generation quickest to adopt new technology. Though a majority of teens still read the Bible in traditional hardcopy form, digital Bible formats are becoming increasingly popular. As youth ministers and leaders across the country continue to invest in the spiritual formation of teens through encouraging Bible reading and engagement, embracing these new technologies and encouraging their use will be central to that goal.
>
> The research also tells us that teens care deeply about the relevance of the Bible to the world in which they inhabit. In a tumultuous political season, many teens believe the Bible can provide moral guidance. The more youth pastors and leaders can make the Bible and its teachings relevant to challenges of today, the more they will simultaneously encourage engagement.[6]

Six years later in one of Barna Research's largest studies (24,870 teens), three key findings stood out:

1. Gen Z may be more open to studying the Bible than we think.
2. Engaging with the Bible has wide-reaching benefits for teenagers.

[6] David Kinnaman quoted in Barna Research, "Top 10 Findings on Teens and the Bible."

3. Teenagers need the adults in their lives to teach them to study the Bible.[7]

Pay close attention to number three. This was one of the most powerful findings—*teenagers who are engaged with the Bible have had an average of four adults teach and model how to study it.* Think about that. Most teens have four grandparents. Imagine if just those four adults told their faith story and the great things that God has done and is doing in our world to each grandchild using the Bible as their guide. The world would be much different.

I have watched several grandchildren (adults now) grow up with our boys. We were blessed to know their grandparents. I asked two of them what advice they would give grandparents. Listen to the words of a grandson (James):

1. Be present whenever possible: This might be true of all grandkids, but I did not realize how blessed I was to have my grandparents until they were gone. Once they were gone, I began to notice the profound influence they had on my life because of their close proximity (presence) and involvement in my life. I imagine being a grandparent can be a thankless job, especially because I was too young to be able to articulate how much I loved my grandparents to them when they were alive. However, the amount of return on investment is nearly incalculable. They gave me many priceless memories, life lessons, intentionally stewarded impressionable moments, and left me with clear examples of what a God fearing/loving grandparent looks like; a gift only they could give.

2. Remember you're all we've got: Grandparents are rare. This was also something I noticed later in life: Most people

[7]Barna Research, "The Open Generation," Barna, 2022, https://www.barna.com/the-open-generation/.

don't have both sets of grandparents, and sometimes they don't have any at all. It's a very special relationship that is all too rare and has awesome potential for lifelong influence.

3. Have tons of fun: One of my favorite characteristics and expectations for grandparents is that they are fun, mostly because mine were very fun. You get to be the "old person" who knows how to have fun, joke around, and be silly. Similar to the rarity of the relationship itself, young kids often don't get to see good examples of older adults (older than their parents) who love God and don't take themselves too seriously. I'm so grateful for the jokes my grandparents played on me, the laughs we shared, and the fun times we had. I will always hold those memories close.

I must point out number one above. *Being there!* Your physical presence in the life of your grandchildren cannot be measured most likely until you are gone and they are grown. Now listen to the words a beautiful granddaughter (Savannah) sent to me:

> I would say the thing that stood out to me the most was that they were so able to get on "our level." They made us feel that they were so genuinely interested in the things that we were interested in—and continued to do so in each phase of our lives. They were aware of current events that affected our age groups and just held so much awareness for what we were each going through individually. They never felt "old school" like stereotypical grandparents, but they always felt current, which made us really love being with them.
>
> They were really intentional about time spent with us and making that time fun. We spent every Thursday afternoon with them and always looked forward to it; we had fun traditions

> that never got boring. We did mystery trips every summer with our cousins. They were just so FUN even though I'm sure we wore them out!
>
> I also recall them incorporating biblical truths into all kinds of things we did, and I think that probably shaped us and were some really instrumental building blocks in our faith, more than we can really understand. Their lives were and are so saturated in Jesus that it seeped into all aspects of their living. For instance . . . we played Bible Jenga instead of regular Jenga.

I love the word "intentional" as she describes "being present" and making it fun. One of the hardest things I try to do is pay attention to what our granddaughters are singing and watching. I am trying to teach them that the 1980s had the best music ever. The fact that the grandparents of the granddaughter above made the effort to be aware of the grandchildren's surroundings resonated highly with her. And she is also right about how it "wears you out." As I write this, our four granddaughters are waking up from spending the night with us. Last night we went to the pool, then we came back and made slime. We ate supper with Uncle Matt and Aunt SaySay. We watched YouTube videos of funny babies, then we read the story of John the Baptist being born, said our prayers, and eventually went to sleep. Tomorrow they will go home, and we will take a nap.

Let me end this short chapter with some advice to grandparents from seven- to ten-year-olds:[8]

---

[8]Peggy Edwards and Mary Jane Sterne, *Intentional Grandparenting: A Contemporary Guide* (Fulcrum Publishing, 2008), 10–11.

The world's greatest grandmother

- Likes to go fishing and makes a lot of good food
- Cuddles with me and has me for sleepovers
- Likes pizza and hanging out the clothes
- Is nice, rich, and works in a candy shop

The world's greatest grandfather

- Is nice, old, tall, and fun (wow!)
- Plays with me and takes me everywhere
- Calls me Twinker
- Climbs trees with me and gives me money

If I could change one thing about my grandmother

- She'd let me stay up later
- She'd stop pinching my cheeks
- She would take us swimming more, and help us build things
- She and my granddad would live together
- I would not change anything; I love her the way she is

If I could change one thing about my grandfather

- He would do more things with me
- We would not go fishing
- He would give me more kisses
- He would not get older
- He would get me a cat
- I would not change anything; I love him the way he is

Reflect and Discuss

1. What is the best piece of advice so far that you have received from any of your grandchildren?
2. How do you react when a grandchild suggests something for you to try?
3. How would you to use the topics in the four lists above with your grandchildren?
4. Have you witnessed Bible literacy going up or down in your family?
5. How can we as a group of grandparents change the decline in Bible literacy?
6 How good is your church at helping your grandchildren become more Bible literate?
7. Have any of your adult children given you advice about how to connect better with your grandchildren?
8. Think about how you might get your younger grandchildren to draw family pictures. (Caution: If you are not a trained psychologist, don't try to overinterpret the drawings. Your grandkid might not be Leonardo da Vinci.)
9. Start a book of all your grandchildren's "art."
10. Draw your faith story for your grandchildren. (Check out narrative art—art that tells a story. Much of Western art until the twentieth century has been narrative, depicting stories from religion, myth and legend, history and literature.)

CHAPTER ELEVEN

Creating a Legacy

"Legacy" tends to get our attention as we get older. We have time to reflect on our lives, and many wonder if they will be remembered, if they made a difference in the world, and what they are leaving behind. This chapter looks at many of the answers we received from grandparents on these topics. Suggestions for those who need help in this area are included.

Remember

A man once told me to put my hand in a bucket of water, hold it there, then pull it out quickly. He then told me that the time it takes the water to replace where my hand was, that is the time that I would be remembered when I die. Sobering thought. I am optimistic enough to think that I might be remembered a little longer than that—at least by my children and grandchildren. Even very famous people of the past are often eventually forgotten. Do you know or remember Thomas Meighan, Norma Talmadge, or Marie Dressler? Maybe some of you reading this book might remember.

These were the most famous movie stars in the 20s and 30s. They were *once* famous. Choose to be famous to your grandchildren right now while you are alive. We do think legacy is very important. Most people probably think about what they are leaving behind as legacy. The fact is, we build our legacy while living. While our goal should be to live well, we will not live forever. We should create something that will live forever. How we live our lives right now, today, will far outweigh what we leave behind when we are dead.

"Legacy" basically means "something that is passed on" and can be presented in several different ways:

- Legacies may be of your faith, ethics, and core values.
- Legacies may be monetary or your assets.
- Legacies may come from your character, reputation, and the life you lead—setting an example for others and to guide their futures.
- Legacies often tremendously impact, encourage, and leave pathways for future generations.
- Legacies provide guidance and inspiration for family members and those impacted by you to live lives that impact their faith, homes, community, and businesses.

Notice that even the legal lawyer definition of "legacy" includes faith. In an *Aging Well* study by the Barna Group, participants said it was important to leave a legacy, but many of them did not equate this with telling their faith story and telling about the great things God has done and is doing in our world.[1] In the grandparent study, participants felt that leaving a legacy was important and chose "loving God and loving others" (32 percent), "being a good example" (27 percent), and "being faithful" (14 percent), as the top three legacies to leave behind to their grandchildren.

[1]Matthew Leighty, *Aging Well* (Barna Group, 2023).

I also asked the grandparents what legacy their grandparents left them. "Being faithful to God and church" (46 percent), "family ties" (9 percent), and "loving God and loving others" (17 percent) were the top three answers.

Legacy might be defined as the positive impact that one has had on their family and friends. (When people think about you, what do they remember about you?) Legacy could be money or property left to someone in a will. When I think about legacy, I usually think about sports figures, or musicians, or politicians, and in my world of Christian ministry, I think about people who have been influencers in our faith tradition. When I hear the word "legacy" sometimes I think: Will it last? We give awards every year at our children's and youth ministries conference (www.ncym.org). These awards are named after some great pioneering people in ministry. Most of the people receiving these awards never met these pioneers. Except for what we tell them, they know nothing about them. We are attempting to keep their legacy alive—to remember. One of the awards even has the word "legacy" in the title. The awards are to remind the conference attendees and recipients of the hard work and dedication the namesake put into forging ministry to young people in our faith tradition—and to do likewise.

In Joshua 4:1–7, Joshua sets up a place to remember:

> When the whole nation had finished crossing the Jordan, the Lord said to Joshua, "Choose twelve men from among the people, one from each tribe, and tell them to take up twelve stones from the middle of the Jordan, from right where the priests are standing, and carry them over with you and put them down at the place where you stay tonight."
>
> So Joshua called together the twelve men he had appointed from the Israelites, one from each tribe, and said

> to them, "Go over before the ark of the LORD your God into the middle of the Jordan. Each of you is to take up a stone on his shoulder, according to the number of the tribes of the Israelites, to serve as a sign among you. In the future, when your children ask you, 'What do these stones mean?' tell them that the flow of the Jordan was cut off before the ark of the covenant of the LORD. When it crossed the Jordan, the waters of the Jordan were cut off. These stones are to be a memorial to the people of Israel forever."

Working on this chapter reminds me of why I originally started thinking about doing this grandparent study. Why did Israel forget? How could they forget in one generation? Maybe one stack of twelve stones was not enough. Maybe walking through the Red Sea on dry ground was not impressive enough. Eating quail biscuits every morning didn't do it either. Right before Moses dies in Deuteronomy, he teaches the Israelites a song and tells them that the words of the song are their very life. They swear they will never forget them—but they do, over and over again. "Remember the Alamo!" I doubt many of today's students outside of Texas even know what that means or where it is. We have taken our youth groups to Gettysburg and to the Tomb of the Unknown Soldier and to the Vietnam Veterans Memorial. We have been to Auschwitz and Birkenau. All those memorials are supposed to help us remember. Yet, we still have war. We forget.

Jesus gathers some brothers and sisters around a table and has the Jewish Passover meal with them. He takes two familiar items—wine and bread—and tells the group, essentially, "Every time you eat and drink these items that are my body and blood of the new covenant, remember me." If you grew up going to church, most likely there was a table for Communion (Lord's Supper, Eucharist) in the church that had the words "Do This in Remembrance of Me" inscribed across the front panel.

People were asked who has left the biggest legacies in the world. Answers were Albert Einstein, Martin Luther King Jr., Mother Teresa, Nelson Mandela, Marie Curie, William Shakespeare, and Queen Elizabeth, followed by several sports figures and movie stars. I don't think I have ever seen the name Jesus Christ in any of those lists. Yet it is most difficult to believe that he has not been one of the biggest (whether you like him or not) influencers in the world. The cross is probably one of the most recognized symbols in the world. Vicki and I have been to over one hundred countries. We always look for a cathedral or church, and we can say firsthand that there are crosses in or on all of them. Another symbol that helps us to remember.

So back to legacy. How you live now in front of your grandchildren will be your legacy. You might leave them some money or property, but they will remember the relationship they have with you and how you treated them and other people. Jesus was correct when he said the greatest command is to love God, and the second greatest command is to love others as yourself. Our children and grandchildren are watching us. In our survey we asked what legacy respondents want to leave their grandchildren; see Figure 11.1 below.

Legacy You Are Leaving Your Grandchildren

	Frequency	Percent
Love God, love others	229	31.7
Good example	197	27.2
None	5	0.7
Supporting family	37	5.1
Jesus/God most important	60	8.3

	Frequency	Percent
Not sure	36	5.0
Love nature	1	0.1
Go to church	16	2.2
Be faithful	100	13.8
Do more spiritual things	2	0.3
Stick to the Bible	7	1.0
Servant	8	1.1
Trust God	12	1.7
Trust yourself / think for yourself	3	0.4
Prayer	2	0.3
Be accountable to God	1	0.1
Sharing Christ	6	0.8
Good name	1	0.1
Totals	**723**	**100%**

Figure 11.1

Legacy Your Grandparents Left You

	Frequency	Percent
Love God, love others	126	16.9
Faithfulness to God and church	344	46.2
Family ties	69	9.3
None/bad	131	17.6
Being a member of the Church of Christ	8	1.1
Love nature and outdoors	2	0.3
Work ethic / learn more	65	8.7
Totals	**745**	**100%**

Figure 11.2

Notice in the table that 32 percent of our grandparent participants chose "Love God, love others" to be their legacy. Another

27 percent chose "good example." These two were above all the others. These are good choices because they require relationships. We hoped more would choose "Sharing Christ" (telling your faith story and the great things that God has done and is doing in our world). We also asked our grandparent participants what legacy their grandparents left them. Figure 11.2 shows the answers they gave. "Love God, love others" (17 percent) was the third-highest choice. Notice "none or bad" (18 percent) was second highest choice, with "faithfulness to God and church" (46 percent) first. This was an interesting finding. Almost half of our study participants chose "faithfulness to God and church" as a legacy that their grandparents left them. Notice in Figure 11.1, "be faithful" is only mentioned as a legacy by less than 14 percent of the grandparent study participants.

Looking at the current statistics of church dropouts and the "nones," there might be a connection here. My baby boomer generation has not done a good job of endearing faithfulness to God and the church to millennials and Gen Zers (our children and grandchildren). Good news—if you are still alive, you have time. (Stop reading this book and go tell your faith story and the good things God has done and is doing in our world—now!)

Our faith community is vital to the legacy of our faith story. We need the church as it was meant to be by its founder (Jesus). Many people find brotherhood, sisterhood, support, and resources in their church. As we have watched so many walk away from the church, we have to ask, "Why?" There are several reasons that can be found in research studies. Here are a few I heard when editing a book about teenagers owning their own faith:[2]

- Their faith was never really theirs in the first place.

---

[2] Dudley Chancey and Ron Bruner, *Owning Faith: Reimagining the Role of Church and Family in the Faith Journey of Teenagers* (Abilene Christian University Press, 2017).

- They are turned off by hypocrisy among Christians (especially their parents).
- No one discipled them after their baptism or confirmation.
- Culture dictates that they can live differently than their Christian upbringing has taught them.
- The adults aren't listening. Adults are answering questions young people are not asking.
- They have had no real grounding in the Bible.
- They have a better community outside the church.

About five years ago Vicki and I planted some trees in our backyard. We did much YouTube searching on how to plant a tree so that it would actually live and grow. We had planted some before in Tennessee, only to watch them die. I am happy to say that in five years, these trees are beautiful (surviving one ice storm) and provide great shade in the summer months. While researching trees, I found some notes about trees that reminded me of the importance of like-minded support not only for our grandchildren, but also for us. Trees like to be in close groups. They thrive better together. They share food resources and help each other survive. Their root systems interlock, providing more stability.[3]

Who knew? The church should be a place like a forest. I think this is another example of my generation not telling their children and grandchildren the great things God has done and is doing in our world. Many people aren't seeing or feeling the connection to the church. We must do better. Our lives are connected by stories. We are narrative people. We need to be about telling our faith story and the great things God has done and is doing in our world.

---

[3] "Tree Size Matters: Why Planting Bigger Is Not Better," Choose Natives, https://choosenatives.org/articles/tree-size-matters-why-planting-bigger-is-not-better/.

Tell your grandchildren your life story. Explain to them how your faith guided you to make the decisions you have made throughout your life. Be open and honest. Your children and grandchildren will appreciate and love you and remember you for being real and authentic. When we talk about leaving a legacy, it's more than leaving stuff. It's our story.

Research studies with older people have found that leaving a legacy is more about passing on values and beliefs ahead of material possessions.[4] Money is not a legacy. The financial inheritance families receive, whether large or small, is gone in an average of seventeen months. David Green, founder of Hobby Lobby, in his book *Giving It All Away* stated only about 30 percent of family businesses survive into the next generation.[5]

Legacy provides a satisfying end to one's "life story" and an ability to influence others long after one's death.[6] Even in these secular articles we see the word "story" over and over again. Remember, one of the purposes of this book is to get us to tell our faith story to our children and grandchildren. In the next few pages are some examples and prompts to help you write it and tell it.

An Ethical Will

Rabbi Steve Leder, in his book *For You When I Am Gone*, helps readers to tell their story.[7] This is a very old Jewish tradition where

---

[4]Elizabeth G. Hunter, "Beyond Death: Inheriting the Past and Giving to the Future, Transmitting the Legacy of One's Self," *Omega (Westport)* 56, no. 4 (2007): 313–29.

[5]David Green with Bill High, *Giving It All Away . . . and Getting It All Back Again* (Zondervan, 2017), 26.

[6]Brett Waggoner, Jesse M. Bering, and Jamin Halberstadt, "The Desire to Be Remembered: A Review and Analysis of Legacy Motivations and Behaviors," *New Ideas in Psychology* 69 (2022).

[7]Steve Leder, *For You When I Am Gone: 12 Essential Questions to Tell a Life Story* (Avery, 2022), 5–240.

a document was created to stand alongside the material will as the father shares life lessons with his son, and in doing so, he passes on his values (ethical will). Think about how you would answer these questions—to pass on to your children and grandchildren. The twelve questions are:

1. What do you regret?
2. When was a time you led with your heart?
3. What makes you happy?
4. What was your biggest failure?
5. What got you through your greatest challenge?
6. What is a good person?
7. What is love?
8. Have you ever cut someone out of your life?
9. How do you want to be remembered?
10. What is good advice?
11. What will your epitaph say?
12. What will your final blessing be?

Tough questions here. Where do these fit in your faith story?

A Legacy Letter—A Type of Ethical Will

Perhaps an easier task for some would be to write a legacy letter, which is a type of an ethical will. This type of letter documents lessons you have learned from life, the values you cherish, and any other experiences that you believe will benefit your children and grandchildren to know about. This doesn't have to be a book, just a few pages where you share wisdom and knowledge gained from years of living out your story. We have seen examples of these letters that included everything from a life history to family recipes. The point here for us is that you combine all the topics in your letter to culminate into your faith story. This is what is most important. Here is a list to get you started:

Awards and honors	Family recipes	Sibling relationships
Values	Hopes and dreams	Schooling
Your best memories	Sports, clubs, etc.	Your history
Work and career	Community involvement	Health history

As an alternative in this age of technology, you could do this as a video recording. (This is especially cool if you are older and have the possibility of having more grandchildren after you are gone. They get to see you and meet you.)

Leave a Lasting Legacy

The caretakers at Dakota Home Care help their clients produce a lasting legacy—a narrative (story) of wisdom and a collection of contributions that endure through the ages. They use the following to craft this lasting legacy:

- **Pass Down Family Traditions:** Family traditions are the threads that weave through generations, connecting individuals across time. Whether it's a secret recipe, a holiday tradition, or a cultural custom, these elements contribute to a legacy that reflects the essence of family identity.
- **Create a Family Tree:** Building a family tree is a tangible and visual representation of your lineage. Older adults can lead in researching and documenting family history, tracing ancestry, and creating a family tree, providing a sense of connection and continuity for future generations.
- **Foster Intergenerational Connections:** Actively engaging with younger generations fosters a sense of connection and understanding. Older adults can create opportunities for intergenerational bonding through shared activities, storytelling sessions, or mentorship programs.

- **Establish a Philanthropic Legacy:** For those passionate about making a positive impact on the community, establishing a philanthropic legacy is a meaningful avenue. Whether through charitable donations, endowments, or active involvement in community projects, older adults can leave a lasting imprint on causes dear to their hearts.
- **Share Life Lessons and Wisdom:** Crafting a legacy involves sharing the wealth of wisdom accumulated over a lifetime. Older adults can actively engage in conversations with family members, friends, and community members, offering guidance and sharing life lessons.
- **Document Personal Values and Principles:** Identifying and documenting personal values and principles contributes to a legacy of integrity and character. This legacy of values serves as a foundation for ethical decision-making and moral growth.
- **Create a Digital Legacy:** In the digital age, older adults can extend their legacy into the virtual realm. Creating a digital legacy involves curating online content, recording video messages, or even establishing a presence on social media platforms to share reflections, stories, and insights.[8]

We would add to this list—your faith story. Please tell your children and grandchildren!

Build a Spiritual Legacy

These ideas were specifically given to create a legacy-type will, totally based off mandates in Scripture such as Deuteronomy

[8] "How to Leave a Lasting Legacy for Generations to Come," Dakota Home Care, January 9, 2024, https://dakotahomecare.com/how-to-leave-a-lasting-legacy-for-generations-to-come/.

6:4–9—the Shema. The idea is to include the Bible in everything we do and say. The values and truths in Scripture are there for a reason—use them! Pick and choose from all the ideas in this chapter. You don't have to do everything. The main goal of this chapter is to encourage you to do something today. I have edited the following thirteen ideas from Crosswalk:[9]

- **Hide his Word**—Memorize Scripture as a family.
- **Talk about justice**—We should fight for justice around us because our God is just.
- **Foster an attitude of gratitude**—Develop a family "gratitude prompt" by deciding together what everyday sight or sound will remind you to thank God for his many gifts.
- **Point to God's purposes**—Talk with your children and grandchildren about the gifts and talents God has given them.
- **Focus on missions**—Take your family on a mission trip (to Honduras with Dudley).
- **Do spiritual "checkups"**—Establish a regular time to talk individually with your children and grandchildren about their relationship with God.
- **Foster servant hearts**—As a family, identify some physical needs in your community. Brainstorm ways you could meet one or more of them together.
- **Build an unshakeable faith**—Tough times can shake our faith. Make a list of biblical truths to keep on hand for the difficult days when you and your family will need them.
- **Establish some "spiritual markers"**—Memorialize a mighty work of God in your family by connecting the story to a unique physical object.

[9] Kathy Howard, "13 Practical Tips for Building a Spiritual Legacy," Crosswalk, updated November 2, 2021, https://www.crosswalk.com/family/parenting/practical-tips-for-building-a-spiritual-legacy.html.

- **Write your faith story**—Record your journey of faith for your family today and in the future.
- **Faith camp**—Plan a weekend camp or day camp around a creative theme for your children or grandchildren.
- **Equip for evangelism**—Help your children understand the eternal consequences for people who don't know Jesus.
- **Celebrate Jesus**—As each holiday and family get-together approaches, find creative ways to direct your family's attention to Jesus and his provision.

So, you might be asking, does anyone really do any of these? The answer is yes. I had heard about "Shankcamp." Dr. Harold Shank and his wife Sally do number eleven from the previous list.[10] I asked him to write me a short description of the Shankcamp experience (keep in mind that if you invite others outside of the nuclear family you grew up in, they may not totally get what the goals of the camp are). I hope you will try this:

> While working for Agape in Memphis, we had Dan Garrett[11] come in as a consultant. He reflected on his book *Leaving a Legacy* in which he talked about how most families **pass on their valuables but not their values**. He even had statistics about how those who inherited money without values wasted the money. Since we had sons recently married and now with young children, and as we were approaching our senior years, we wanted to make sure we passed on our values.
>
> Our proposal to these two families was that we would rent a farmhouse and pay almost all the expenses, if the two

---

[10] Dr. Harold Shank is an Old Testament scholar, a professor, a university president, an author of numerous books and commentaries, a husband, a father, and a grandfather. He can be reached at drharoldshank@gmail.com.

[11] Dan T. Garrett and Tim Woodroof, *Leaving a Legacy: Sustaining Family Unity, Faith, and Wealth* (Leafwood Publishers, 2014).

> couples would sit with Sally and Harold for six hours during the event. We would send out questions ahead of time for discussion. Early on, most of the questions came from Garrett's book. They agreed and the results were significant.
>
> We were all thrilled with the result. We got to know our daughters-in-law, we got to see how they were passing on values to their children (our grandchildren), and we as a group wrestled with difficult questions.
>
> All of us participate and answer the questions. Sometimes the questions are about us: What could Harold and Sally as parents and now grandparents do better?
>
> Other activities also take place. Sally holds a children's Bible class. Daniel and Nathan plan events for the grandchildren. The three couples take turns providing the meals. The grandchildren, the cousins, love the event and have become the glue that holds it together. They insist that we do it again.
>
> I led the discussions and Sally took notes. We review the notes each year before we go again. We call the event Shankcamp. Last year the sons and daughters-in-law asked if they could pose the questions for the next Shankcamp. Sally's brother and cousin are also coming and hosting the Shank Olympics in the summer of 2024.

Currently, one of the best Christian grandparenting organizations is Legacy Coalition.[12] They provide great support, programming, and resources for grandparents. They produce a yearly grandparent summit that can be attended in person or simulcasted at several churches around the country. They also do Grand Monday Nights, which is a weekly webinar with special guests providing information and encouragement for grandparents. They

[12] www.legacycoalition.com.

exist to help grandparents have a greater spiritual impact on their families—intentionally!

If our grandchildren are asked one day, "What legacy did your grandparents leave you?" what will they say? The opening line of the book *The Disappearance of Childhood* reads, "Children are the living messages we send to a time we will not see."[13] What message are we sending with them? The leaders of Stewardship Legacy Coaching put it this way: "We must be intentional and authentic in walking out and leaving a godly spiritual legacy. Our legacy is attached to our faith. We cannot leave an effective legacy if our character does not match what we say we believe."[14] They give ideas on their website on how to be godly, biblical, consistent, and intentional.

The apostle Paul said this, "Therefore I, a prisoner for serving the Lord, beg you to lead a life worthy of your calling, for you have been called by God" (Eph. 4:1 NLT). Those of us who are parents and grandparents are called to disciple the next generations. We must be intentional in all we do. For some reason, Joshua didn't get it done. He was a great leader, but all that he did leading Israel went for naught in 722 BC and 586 BC. God's chosen people forgot who chose them.

Remember, your legacy is being built right now, today. Tell your children and grandchildren your faith story and the great things that God has done and is doing in our world!

---

[13] Neil Postman, *The Disappearance of Childhood* (Vintage Books, 1982), xi.

[14] Jeff Rogers, "How to Leave a Godly Spiritual Legacy," Stewardship Legacy Coaching, October 31, 2021, https://stewardshiplegacy.com/how-to-leave-a-godly-spiritual-legacy/.

Reflect and Discuss

1. Do you have some type of ethical will? If not, use some of the ideas in this chapter to create one. Think of it as your last will and testament, but from the spiritual side of life.
2. What would it look like in your family to have a week together in the mountains or at the beach mainly to talk about spiritual legacies?
3. Why do you think that one generation after Joshua forgot God?
4. Are we repeating what happened in Joshua and Judges today? If so, how?
5. How can you be more intentional in building your legacy today for your grandchildren?
6. Teach your grandchildren some easy Bible verses that communicate values they need in their lives. Make a list of those today.
7. How can you help your children with the legacy they are leaving their children (your grandchildren)?
8. What is the most difficult thing for you to accomplish in leaving a legacy today? How can you get help with that?
9. If you died today, what would your grandchildren remember about you?
10. Go tell your faith story and the great things that God has done and is doing in our world.

CHAPTER TWELVE

Support for Grandparents

If one puts "support for grandparents" into Google, they will get over 154 million hits. Most of them are about grandparents raising grandchildren and the help they can get raising grandchildren. In other chapters, I have mentioned some support that grandparents can get in certain contexts. This short chapter will highlight other sources of help and support for issues grandparents may face. There are excellent websites dedicated to serving grandparents.

A few areas that might be of interest to you or your friends are listed here:

- Adoption
- Care and Custody
- Networks
- Education
- Federal Laws
- Financial Assistance
- Guardianship Assistance
- Kinship Publications
- National Family Caregiver Support
- National Organizations
- Healthcare
- Housing

All these areas are listed under resources at www.grandfamilies.org along with other areas. "Grand Facts" is a very good resource on this site. When you click on the link, you get a map of the USA. Find your state and click on it. You will get several pages of information for grandparents including phone numbers, websites, and information. A most excellent website for grandparents.

I am sure that most of you reading this have received an invite to AARP. The American Association of Retired Persons is one of the largest membership organizations in the world. Millions of people are making a difference for people fifty years and older. There is power in numbers. Take a brief look around www.aarp.org, and you will realize the massive efforts being made for older people. AARP was founded by a retired school teacher—don't ever think that you cannot make a difference in the world.[1] Just in case you need a refresher:

> AARP is the nation's largest nonprofit, nonpartisan organization dedicated to empowering Americans 50 and older to choose how they live as they age. With a nationwide presence, AARP strengthens communities and advocates for what matters most to the more than 100 million Americans 50-plus and their families: health and financial security, and personal fulfillment. . . . As a trusted source for news and information, AARP produces the nation's largest circulation publications, *AARP The Magazine* and *AARP Bulletin*.[2]

AARP is inexpensive to join, and the benefits and discounts pay back your membership. The website is always up-to-date with helpful support and information. There are offices in all fifty states, with the national office being in Washington, DC, right where

---

[1]Craig Walker, *Ethel Percy Andrus: One Woman Who Changed America* (AARP, 2018).

[2]"What Is AARP?" AARP, February 19, 2025, https://help.aarp.org/s/article/what-is-aarp.

policies are enacted. AARP advocates for older people by fighting for health security, for financial security, and to protect consumers. Each of these areas are described in detail on the AARP website. The AARP is definitely a very helpful support for grandparents and other older people in our country. Along with the AARP, below are some other membership organizations you might want to check out.

AMAC—Association of Mature American Citizens

AMAC (amac.us) was founded in 2007 and is a much younger organization than AARP. However, like the better-known AARP, it is devoted to providing benefits for and improving the lifestyle of seniors. They promote low-cost and affordable insurance and a wide array of discounts. These discounts may vary from those offered by the AARP, which is why seniors join both organizations—for a full assortment of benefits. The AMAC differs from AARP in one critical detail—it promotes itself as the conservative's alternative to the AARP. They advocate for traditional American values, such as faith, family, and freedom as a political platform. Their bi-monthly magazine is geared toward "patriotic Americans" and the role the government should be playing in their lives. Like the AARP, AMAC offers its members many discounts, including travel, dental, vision, auto loans, etc. The goal is to help seniors save money in all areas of life.

National Council on Aging

The National Council on Aging (NCOA—ncoa.org) is "promoting vital aging in America." The NCOA's affiliated organizations are agencies on aging, senior centers, long-term health care facilities, churches, employment services, and others with the ability to help seniors over fifty. The council assists seniors—especially low-income seniors—with the Supplemental Nutrition Assistance Program (SNAP) to help seniors eat more and healthier, along with the Low-Income Home Energy Assistance Program. NCOA has partnered with the National Association of Area Agencies on Aging (usaging.org) to spread the word and educate the public on the abundance of benefits that they may be missing. Their motto is, "You Gave, Now Save." The NCOA advocates for self-care and positive mental health for caregivers who may be experiencing a great deal of isolation and loneliness.

Family Caregiver Alliance

Many seniors rely on caregivers to help them live more independently in their own homes instead of being forced into a senior facility. Everyone has their concerns about the elderly, but what about the caregiver? More than fifty-three million Americans provide care to family, friends, and neighbors. Most realize that helping someone else live a better life is rewarding, but sometimes the caretaker needs to take care of himself or herself. The FCA provides that support.[3]

Red Hat Society

The Red Hat Society is not limited to women over fifty, but the great majority of members are seniors.[4] It is a social organization that encourages senior women to socialize while wearing a purple outfit with a red hat—the larger, the better. Older women can suffer from isolation, especially single women and those without families. They have become invisible. The Red Hat Society

---

[3] https://www.caregiver.org.

[4] Bridget Reed Morawski, "What Is the Red Hat Society?," *U.S. News & World Report*, August 4, 2022, https://money.usnews.com/money/retirement/aging/articles/what-is-the-red-hat-society.

sponsors outings, from visits to museums to luncheons to movies, encouraging women to get out and make friends.

Grandparents Rights and Other Issues That Need Support

Divorce and death are the two main reasons that grandparents lose connections with their grandchildren. The side that gets custody of the grandchildren especially in divorce situations can become very guarded and possessive of the grandchildren, depriving grandparents access to their grandchildren. Grandparents have been taking legal action to be able to see their grandchildren. Grandparents Rights Organization (www.grandparentsrights.org) is a nonprofit that exists to: "Educate and support grandparents and grandchildren and to advocate their desire to continue a relationship that may be threatened with loss of contact or amputation, usually following: family acrimony; a child being born out of wedlock; the death of one of the child's parents or the divorce of the grandchild's parents."

When the grandparents in the Grandparent Project study were asked if anything kept them from seeing their grandchildren, only thirty (3 percent) replied "yes." They were asked if they had direct communication with their grandchildren any time they wanted to, and 93 percent said that they did. Other areas in the study where grandparents might need support are listed here:

- Eighty-eight of the participants said divorce and marriage issues affected their relationships with their grandchildren. Half of these (50 percent) said these issues affected them "a lot" and "too much."
- Seventy-six of the participants said church splits and church problems affected their relationships with their

grandchildren. Over half of these (58 percent) said these issues affected them "a lot" and "too much."

- Twenty of the participants were struggling with SSA/LGBTQ/trans issues that affected their relationships with their grandchildren. Over half of these (55 percent) said these issues affected them "a lot" and "too much."

Divorce

Divorce is messy. Grandparents can be a tremendous help with their adult children and grandchildren during these times. Someone must keep a level head. Emotions run high. Here are some tips to help navigate these times.[5] Check out the website for more details.

- Make your home a secure, safe place. Stick with familiar routines for things like meals and bedtimes.
- Keep doing things that you and your grandchild like to do together.
- Listen when your grandchild wants to talk about their thoughts, feelings, and fears. This can help you work out how best to comfort them.
- Always speak respectfully about both of your grandchild's parents and avoid taking sides.
- Try to maintain a good relationship with your child's ex-partner if possible.
- If you experience any conflict with your grandchild's parents, make sure that your grandchild isn't involved.
- Try to be positive with your grandchild about their family's future.

---

[5] "When Your Grandchild's Parents Divorce," RaisingChildren.net, last updated September 26, 2024, https://raisingchildren.net.au/grown-ups/grandparents/family-relationships/when-parents-divorce.

Church Problems

Many church people find support within their community of faith—their church. Church politics, church problems, and church splits can upset faith. It is hard not to find support there, of all places. It is sad that this affected some of the participants in the Grandparent Project. It is even more sad when some end up not going back to a church at all. After all, church, faith, God, Jesus—this was the emphasis of the Grandparent Project. If grandparents have their faith shattered by these issues, their faith story may become unimportant to them. In fact, some might even steer their grandchildren away from this thing called church. This gets tough if it is the church you grew up in—your home church.

One of the last things Jesus thought and prayed about was unity.[6] There are usually plenty of churches to choose from in most cities. If church is getting toxic for you, find another one to attend. Ask the leaders to bring in a mediator if needed to settle things before they become toxic. Remember that Christ died for the church. Don't be part of breaking one up. Take the high road. In the end, churches and faith-based organizations become a much-needed support[7] for grandparents and other older people.[8]

Sexual Identity Issues

Where do grandparents go for support when they have an adult child "come out," or they find out they have a same-sex attracted (SSA), gay or lesbian (LGBTQIA+), or trans grandchild? This is

---

[6] John 17:20–23.

[7] Susan L. Neely-Barnes, J. Carolyn Graff, and Gregory Washington, "The Health-Related Quality of Life of Custodial Grandparents," *Health and Social Work* 35, no. 2 (2010): 87–97.

[8] Tina L. Peterson, "Support and Satisfaction: Perspectives of Older Grandparent Caregivers about Faith-Based Communities," *Journal of Gerontology Social Work* 65, no. 8 (2022): 883–97.

very difficult for most religious people, especially if their views are very conservative.

This is a hot topic in our country and around the world. I was asked to write a chapter for a secular book on "How the Church Treats the LGBT Community."[9] I interviewed twenty-five people who fell into the three categories above. There were a couple of good stories, but most were bad. All the twenty-five but one grew up in the church loving God and Jesus. Most of the twenty-four tried to stay at the church they had grown up in, but when people found out about their different lifestyle, things became too toxic for them to stay. At the time of the interviews, eighteen of them were still attending an affirming church, and two of them were attending the church they grew up in with limited participation allowed.

Support for grandparents dealing with these issues can be difficult if you are starting from scratch. Much of all our identities is being shaped by technology. Imagine being a teenager and asking Google if it is okay to experiment with identity changes. This is happening every minute of the day in our country. So where do you start? I will step out here to say that two of my go-to sources are Dr. Mark Yarhouse[10] and Dr. Walt Mueller.[11] We have had both men at our national children's and youth minister's conference.[12] Please visit their websites and read about all their resources and research on these timely topics. Remember, you as a grandparent can be a very helpful listening ear to your child or grandchild who may be going through these changes.

---

[9] Dudley Chancey, "How the Church Treats the LGBT Community," in *Gender, Sexual Identity, and Families: The Personal Is Political*, ed. Kevin P. Lyness and Judith L. Fisher (Michigan Publishing Services, 2019).

[10] https://www.wheaton.edu/academics/faculty/mark-yarhouse/.

[11] https://www.cpyu.org.

[12] https://www.ncym.org.

Become Aware of All Your State Has to Offer You and Your Grandchildren

Each state has different helps and support for grandparents. Here is one example from the state of Tennessee: www.kidcentraltn.com. Go to this website and click on the links to get more specifics about each topic. When different life events happen, there is so much to know and learn to take care of a grandchild. Check your state to see if they have something like this.

If you are a part-time caregiver or full-time guardian of your grandchild, think about childproofing your home, finding out car seat requirements, learning the ABC's of a child's sleep environment, and general information about the development stages children pass through.

One of our intentional things we do with our grandchildren is reading. We read the Bible at night when they spend the night. We read story books to them during the day. My wife Vicki has a special box that says on top "Read a book, get a prize." So the grandchildren love that box. It's important to read to young children for about twenty minutes each day. But how can busy grandparents help their grandchildren get the most out of story time? Research shows that there is a major literacy crisis in the United States.[13] It is critical that our grandchildren learn to read well. Check out the Internet for your state to get some tips that will help get you started reading to young children.[14] My grandchildren all live in Oklahoma. Oklahoma has an excellent early

---

[13] Allison Rose Socol, "The Literacy Crisis in the US Is Deeply Concerning—and Totally Preventable," *EdTrust* blog, January 17, 2024, https://edtrust.org/blog/the-literacy-crisis-in-the-u-s-is-deeply-concerning-and-totally-preventable/.

[14] For example, here's an organization in Tennessee: "How to Read to Young Children," kidcentral tn, accessed October 15, 2024, https://www.kidcentraltn.com/content/kidcentral/education/reading/how-to-read-to-young-children--.html.

childhood program website.[15] Check out the child development website for your state.

Other areas that state websites address that are helpful in raising grandchildren include relative caregiver programs, helping children get through difficult times, and fun things to do with grandchildren. A good example of fun activities can be found at Kidcentral TN's website.[16]

Other Types of Support for Grandparents

Grandparents who have good social support (clubs, church, and other activities involving people) and good coping skills are more satisfied with their lives and life situations than those who don't. Grandparents who have support groups to lean on have better emotional support. These support systems may be even more important when grandparents are faced with grandchildren with disabilities and life-threatening diseases. One study reported the following concerning grandparents with grandchildren with disabilities:

> Findings indicated that grandparents' involvement and satisfaction with their role were a function of their attitudes towards disabilities in children in general and their relationship with their adult children, as well as their own life experiences. Their involvement with their grandchild with developmental disability served to strengthen the relationship between the grandparents. An important implication of the study is that professionals should plan interventions to

[15] "Early Childhood Program," Oklahoma State Department of Health, accessed April 24, 2025, https://oklahoma.gov/health/health-education/children---family-health/maternal-and-child-health-service/child-and-adolescent-health/early-childhood-.html.

[16] "Fun Activities to Try with Your Kids," Kidcentral TN, accessed February 13, 2025, https://www.kidcentraltn.com/health/physical-activity/fun-activities-to-try-with-your-kids.html.

> support and encourage grandparents to be more involved in the care of the child with developmental disability.[17]

Another study about grandchildren with cancer reported six different themes that surfaced connected with grandchildren diagnosed with cancer: "(a) Diagnosis: changing everything; (b) Aspects of treatment: a different world; (c) Sandwich generation; (d) Family: worrying about everyone; (e) Balancing work; and (f) It's like suddenly a door opens." The study demonstrated "the life-changing impact of having a grandchild diagnosed with cancer" and the importance of family and social support.[18]

So how do you go about telling your faith story and the great things God has done and is doing in our world when you have a grandchild born with disabilities, or a grandchild diagnosed with cancer, or the death of a grandchild? Where is God? Our youngest son had cancer in the middle of his senior year of high school. It rocked our world. For a few weeks we did not know what type of cancer it was. This may surprise you, but I wasn't sitting around talking about my faith and the great things that God had done in our world. I was thinking more on the lines of "why me" and "why him." He has been cancer-free for over ten years. It is easy now talking about how good God is. I mention our story just to say, as we looked back as a family, we were so blessed by our church family and our kin families. Our son had amazing support from teens in our church youth group. They are best friends today as adults. The support was amazing. You get so wrapped up in the moment and in your own stuff that you do not realize who is holding you up and supporting you.

---

[17] Shira Katz and Louise Kessel, "Grandparents of Children with Developmental Disabilities: Perceptions, Beliefs, and Involvement in Their Care," *Comprehensive Pediatric Nursing* 25, no. 2 (2002): 113–28.

[18] Jenny Davies, Moira O'Connor, Georgia K. B. Halkett, Lauren Kelada, and Nicholas G. Gottardo, "Grandparents' Experiences of Childhood Cancer: A Qualitative Study," *Journal of Family Nursing* 30, no. 1 (2024): 30–40.

As much as I dislike what technology is doing to our children (and us), there are some great things about it. If you find yourself or a grandparent friend in need of support, check out the services in your city and state. Go online and Google it. There is help and support out there.

Reflect and Discuss

1. Make a list of help and support hotlines and websites and put it on a wall or fridge.
2. Who or what are some of the best help or support agencies you have dealt with? Share those.
3. Are you one of those people who doesn't like to ask for help?
4. What are some ways you could help young people (your grandchildren) learn how to help older people?
5. Would you be willing to take your grandchildren to an assisted living facility and meet some older people?
6. What are some ways that you could help support older people?
7. Would you be willing to start a support group at your church or club to help older people?
8. How could your church be more involved in supporting the elderly? (James 1:27)
9. Would you be willing to write your congressperson to advocate for support for the elderly?
10. Start a support group that specifically gives grandparents raising grandchildren a break for a couple of hours a week.

CHAPTER THIRTEEN

A Closing Word

If you have read this far, thank you! I do believe I have learned a few things doing this Grandparent Project. I am even more encouraged to "keep the faith" and to share my faith story not only with my grandchildren but with others young and old that God puts in my path.

I was hoping for a little more positive results in the survey as to grandparents actively sharing their faith story and the great things that God has done and is doing in our world. I think from asking the grandparents in the study about their grandparents, one can see a pattern of transmission (or non-transmission) of faith and faith practices. So, this project was not meant to be a condemning or finger-pointing endeavor. I hope that it has been enlightening and even a bit educational as far as learning what others do to share their faith with their grandchildren.

As mentioned in Chapter One, this project developed out of my study of the book of Hosea, preparing for a lecture series in Hawaii, March 2024. Israel (Northern Kingdom) split off from

Judah after refusing to pay higher taxes. They were very blessed for a few years and forgot where those blessings came from. They broke most of the laws of the covenant. They took advantage of people less fortunate. Even the priests became corrupt. Hosea begged them for over forty years to turn back to God and keep the covenant laws. Within two hundred years, they were wiped off the map, never to be heard from again. Remember, this was part of God's chosen people. They were so absorbed in themselves that they forgot where it all came from and that they were supposed to tell their children and grandchildren about the great things that God had done (the Exodus) and was doing in their world.

I see parallels between Israel and where I live. We are very blessed. We have worked hard and sacrificed much (including our families many times) to obtain the dream. We forget many times where it all came from. We get busy and do not have much time to share our faith story and the great things that God has done and is doing in our world.

My hopes and prayers are that we have been reminded about the importance of telling the next generation, starting with our children and grandchildren. God bless you as you do that!

Blessings,
Dudley (April 2025)

Appendix

(The following is taken from the dissertation project of Leon Sanderson of Memphis, Tennessee. Used with permission.)

The Most Important Value to Share—Faith!

A. Objectives

1. To develop an awareness of God and his care/love/grace, creating an ability to trust him.
2. To begin to build faith in Christ who gave himself for the world and set the stage for trust and a grateful obedient response.

B. These last three lessons will have one goal: to intentionally make an effort to teach, coach, and mentor values that, from the teacher and grandparent perspective, are valuable for everyday living and ultimately eternal life.

C. The core value of faith strengthens in this life and leads to eternal life hereafter. Self-discipline and compassion may have an eternal effect, yet faith is a deeper value, underlying all other values.

1. It supports when the going gets rough (cf. Heb. 11:1).
2. It sustains because of the object of faith—God.
3. It involves a dependency upon the Lord as it takes its strength from outside oneself.

I. Theology Supporting This Value

A. Psalmist prayed: "Even when I am old and gray, do not forsake me, my God, till I declare your power to the next generation, your mighty acts to all who are to come" (Ps. 71:18).

1. What can be learned from this passage?
    a. Recognition that the aging process is underway for all.
    b. Recognition that something should take place before life is gone.
    c. Awareness that a dependence on God is part of the task.
2. Task for which Psalmist prays has to do with declaring power or passing the baton of trust in God on to generations to come.

B. Paul admonishes Titus: impart spiritual values, even though three generations not mentioned.

1. Older men are to be self-controlled. Why? To "encourage the young men to be self-controlled" (Titus 2:2, 6).
2. Older women are to "train the young women" in several qualities of Christian walk (Titus 2:3–4 ESV).
3. Important message: Grace of God has come to all; teaches "no" to world and "yes" to godly lives (Titus 2:11–13).

C. Consider texts involving Christian formation:

1. Deut. 6:4–12 (intentional, generational training)
2. Matt. 15:17–20 (thoughts, actions come from the heart)
3. Matt. 28:18–20 (training, discipling)
4. Luke 2:52 (fourfold way Jesus grew)
5. John 7:17 (doing precedes understanding)
6. Rom. 12:1–2 (inward change)
7. Gal. 5:16–18, 25 (live by, keep in step with the Holy Spirit)
8. Eph. 4:11–16 (toward maturity in Christ)
9. 2 Pet. 1:2–11 (partnership and participation lead to productivity)

II. This Lesson Is Challenging

A. Godfrey Phillips: "All over the world the Church is only partially succeeding in passing on, alike to its young people and to those who are outside, the faith by which it lives and the distinctive kind of life which that faith produces."

B. Norbert Greinacher and Virgil Elizondo confirm the challenge by calling attention to a time of rapid social change during which the handing on of the faith is acute; survival of church depends on it.

C. Not automatic; does not work by osmosis.

D. Must be done as Paul wrote to Timothy: "Be strong in the grace that is in Christ Jesus. And the things you have heard me say in the presence of many witnesses entrust to reliable people who will also be qualified to teach others" (2 Tim. 2:1–2).

III. How Can We Pass On Faith?

A. Begin with a definition of faith.

1. Writer of Hebrews uses "sure" and "certain" in description, yet it is about that for which we hope though we do not see.
2. "Sure" and "certain" depict the foundation, underpinning of what is unseen; this makes faith real with unseen object. (Illustration: Insurance policy; note from teacher; letter from friend.)
3. Therefore, faith is synonymous with trust involving confidence. (Illustration: Child jumping to father; youth accepting word of parent.)

B. Teach that what you believe does make a difference in the outcome. (Illustration: Residents in path of hurricane.)

C. True faith results in action; failure to act stems from being unsure or uncertain and reflects unbelief or lack of faith.

1. By faith, Noah built a boat (Heb. 11:7).
2. By faith, Abraham moved without knowing where (Heb. 11:8).

IV. Faith in God and His Word Make a Difference

A. Makes a difference in whom you believe or trust.

1. Is "In God We Trust" simply a slogan, a confidence in money, or a true statement about our confidence?
2. The "whom" indicates your dependable source of information and counsel.

B. Makes a difference in choices made.

1. Failure to believe prompts inactivity. (Illustration: When fire alarm sounds, do you wonder who pulled the lever as a prank?

2. Faith must be placed in right sources or incorrect choices will be made. (Illustration: Selection of plays for team based on scouting reports. If incorrect, results will be substandard.)

C. Faith in God begins with model behavior of parent or grandparent.

D. Faith in God grows as God's faithfulness is realized. (Illustration: Rising of the sun. Ps. 113.)

E. When his faithfulness is known, his Word carries more weight in the bigger picture.

F. In a sense, we pass on the opportunity to believe.

V. Principles to Keep in Mind about Passing on Faith

NOTE: This is to be distinguished from passing on a formula or teaching truths of Bible stories and principles; it may be described as assisting spiritual formation.

A. Faith is better "caught" than "taught"; implies importance of example.

B. Faith develops in stages: infant (observed); childlike (imitation); adolescent (struggling, not sure); adult (owned; questions but knows what it believes and why).

C. "The way most people learn to respect Christ is through what they see in the lives of Christians. The best way to teach a person about Christianity is to be a Christian."

D. Passing on the faith requires intentionality.

E. Faith transmission, development of spirituality involves "roots" and "fruits."

1. Roots: grounding; nurture; sense of identity
2. Fruits: manifestations of identity

VI. Proposed Process

A. Begin with foundation of faith.

1. Bible—Word of God; God's nature
2. God revealed—Christ
3. God's help—Holy Spirit
4. God's abundant love for all in Jesus
5. Our response

B. Foundation points toward building, acting upon.

1. God took the first step: grace
2. Submission, trust
3. Obedience, accepting
4. Baptism as an act of submission, faith, and trust
5. Living for, growing in Christ follows

Conclusion:

A. Consider Deut. 6:4–12 as guideline for process.

B. Goal of process is participation in divine nature (2 Pet. 1:2–11) and "until Christ is formed in you" (Gal. 4:19).

Discussion Question

How would you summarize in ten words or less the spirituality you want to pass on?

Activity

A. Develop questions you would ask your grandchild for the purpose of measuring ownership of faith, internalization of faith. (Illustration: Is the Bible from God? Is faith in God important? In what way does having faith change what you do?)

B. Ask questions of grandchildren that will indicate they are taking the importance of faith seriously. (Are you reading one of the Gospels? What is striking to you? How does this affect the choices you make? Is there anything in the text that draws you closer to the Lord?)

Life in General

(Use the following scale to rate yourself)

Strongly Agree   Agree   Neither Agree nor Disagree

Disagree   Strongly Disagree

1. As I grow older, things seem better than I thought they would be.
2. I have gotten more breaks in life than most people I know.
3. I am as happy now as I was when I was younger.
4. These are the best years of my life.
5. I expect some interesting and pleasant things to happen to me in the future.
6. The things I do are as interesting to me as they ever were.
7. I feel old and somewhat tired.
8. I feel my age, but it does not bother me.
9. As I look back on my life, I am satisfied.
10. I have made plans for things I'll be doing a month or a year from now.
11. I sometimes worry so much that I can't sleep.

12. I sometimes feel that life isn't worth living.
14. I am afraid of a lot of things.
15. Life is hard for me much of the time.
16. Most days I have plenty to do.
17. A person must live for today and not worry about tomorrow.

Bibliography

Books about Grandparents and Grandparenting

Anderson, Stephen A., and Ronald M. Sabatelli. *Family Interaction: A Multigenerational Developmental Perspective.* Pearson Education, 2003.

Arber, Sara, and Virpi Timonen. *Contemporary Grandparenting: Changing Family Relationships in Global Contexts.* The Policy Press, 2012.

Bailey, Sandra J., and Bethany L. Letiecq. "Rural Grandparents Raising Grandchildren: Family Caregiving through Crisis, Adaptation, and Advocacy." In *Caring for Each Other: Family Caregiving across the Generations.* Michigan Publishing, 2023.

Bates, James S., Alan C. Taylor, and M. Hunter Stanfield. "Variations in Grandfathering: Characteristics of Involved, Passive, and Disengaged Grandfathers." In *The Role of Grandparents in the 21st Century*, edited by Ann Buchanan and Anna Rotkirch. Routledge, 2020.

Bengtson, Vern L. *Families and Faith: How Religion Is Passed Down Across Generations.* Oxford University Press, 2013.

Bengtson, Vern L., and Merril Silverstein. "How Grandparents Influence the Religiosity of Their Grandchildren: A Mixed-Methods

Study of Three-Generation Families in the United States." In *Grandparenting Practices Around the World*, edited by Virpi Timonen. Policy Press, 2020.

Bly, Stephen and Janet Bly. *The Power of a Godly Grandparent*. Beacon Hill Press, 2003.

Bruner, Ron, and Dana Kennamer Pemberton. *Along the Way: Conversations about Children and Faith*. Abilene Christian University Press, 2015.

Buchanan, Ann, and Anna Rotkirch. *Grandfathers: Global Perspectives*. Macmillan Publishers, 2016.

Burns, Jim. *Doing Life with Your Adult Children: Keep Your Mouth Shut and the Welcome Mat Out*. Zondervan, 2019.

Burr, Wesley R., Loren D. Marks, and Randal D. Day. *Sacred Matters: Religion and Spirituality in Families*. Routledge, 2012.

Carson, Lillian. *The Essential Grandparent*. Health Communications, 1996.

Chancey, Dudley. "How the Church Treats the LGBT Community." In *Gender, Sexual Identity, and Families: The Personal Is Political*, edited by Kevin P. Lyness and Judith L. Fisher. Michigan Publishing Services, 2019.

Chancey, Dudley, and Ron Bruner. *Owning Faith: Reimagining the Role of Church and Family in the Faith Journey of Teenagers*. Abilene Christian University Press, 2017.

Cherlin, Andrew J., and Frank F. Furstenberg Jr. *The New American Grandparent*. Harvard University Press, 1986.

———. *Styles and Strategies of Grandparenting: A Place in the Family, a Life Apart*. Basic Books, 1986.

Clinton, Hillary R. *It Takes a Village*. Simon and Schuster, 1996.

Cloyd, Betty Shannon. *Parents and Grandparents as Spiritual Guides*. Upper Room Books, 2000.

Cohler, Bertram J., and Henry U. Grunebaum. *Mothers, Grandmothers, and Daughters*. John Wiley & Sons, 1981.

Conroy, Donald B., and Charles J. Fahey. "Christian Perspective on the Role of Grandparents." In *Grandparenthood*, edited by Vern L. Bengtson and Joan Robertson. Sage Publishing, 1985.

Coulter, Gordon R., and James W. Thompson. "A Theology of Grandparenting and Generational Faith." In *A Theology of Family Ministries*, edited by Michael Anthony and Michelle Anthony. Broadman & Holman Academic, 2011.

Dodson, Fitzhugh. *How to Grandparent*. Harper & Row, 1981.

Drury, Amanda. *Saying Is Believing: The Necessity of Testimony in Adolescent Spiritual Development.* InterVarsity Press, 2015.

Edgell, Penny. *Religion and Family in a Changing Society.* Princeton University Press, 2006.

Edwards, Peggy, and Mary Jane Sterne. *Intentional Grandparenting: A Contemporary Guide.* Fulcrum Publishing, 2008.

Egan, M. Winston, and Linda Egan. *Grandparenting on Purpose: Fresh Ideas, Activities, and Traditions for Connecting with Grandchildren Near and Far*. WinnPrint Publishing, 2020.

Fomlin, Angela M. "Grandparents' Influences on Grandchildren." In *Handbook on Grandparenthood*, edited by Maximiliane E. Szinovacz. Greenwood Press, 1998.

Fowler, James W. *Stages of Faith: The Psychology of Human Development and the Quest for Meaning*. Harper One Publishing, 1995.

Garrett, Dan T., and Tim Woodroof. *Leaving a Legacy: Sustaining Family Unity, Faith, and Wealth*. Leafwood Publishers, 2014.

Gianturco, Paola. *Grandmother Power: A Global Phenomenon.* Powerhouse Books, 2012.

Gibbons, Judith L., and Regina Fanjul de Marsicovetere. "Grandparenting in Mexico and Central America." In *Grandparents in Cultural Context,* edited by David Shwalb and Ziarat Hossein. Routledge, 2018.

Green, David. *Giving It All Away . . . and Getting It Back Again.* Zondervan, 2017.

Groom, Thomas. "Handing on the Faith." In *Handing on the Faith: The Church's Mission and Challenge*, edited by Robert P. Imbelli. Herder and Herder, 2006.

Gubrium, Jaber F. *Time, Roles, and Self in Old Age*. Human Sciences Press, 1976.

Harper, Cavin. *Courageous Grandparenting: Unshakable Faith in a Broken World*. The Christian Grandparenting Network, 2013.

Hayslip, Bert, Jr., and Julie Hicks Patrick. *Custodial Grandparenting: Individual, Cultural, and Ethnic Diversity*. Springer Publishing Company, 2006.

Herold, Korie. *Grandpa's Story: A Memory and Keepsake Journal for My Family*. Paige Tate and Company, 2021.

Holmen, Mark. *Faith Begins at Home: Grandparents*. Gospel Light, 2014.

———. *Impress Faith on Your Kids*. Randall House, 2011.

Hosier, Helen Kooiman. *Living the Lois Legacy: Passing On a Lasting Faith to Your Grandchildren*. Tyndale House Publishers, 2002.

Kimmel, Tim, and Darcy Kimmel. *Extreme Grandparenting: The Ride of Your Life!* Focus on the Family, 2007.

Kinnaman, David. *The Open Generation*. Barna Group, 2022.

Kivnick, Helen Q. *The Meaning of Grandparenthood*. UMI Research Press, 1982.

Kornhaber, Arthur. *Contemporary Grandparenting*. Sage Publishing, 1996.

———. *The Grandparent Solution: How Parents Can Build a Family Team for Practical, Emotional, and Financial Success*. Jossey-Bass, 2004.

Kornhaber, Arthur, and Kenneth L. Woodward. *Grandparents/Grandchildren: The Vital Connection*. Transaction Publishers, 1991.

Krause, Corinne Azen. *Grandmothers, Mothers, and Daughters: Oral Histories of Three Generations of Ethnic American Women*. Twayne Publishers, 1991.

Lahey, Jessica. *The Gift of Failure: How the Best Parents Learn to Let Go So Their Children Can Succeed*. Harper Publishing, 2016.

Leighty, Matthew. *Aging Well*. Barna Group, 2023.

Lewis, Phillip V., and John P. Harrison. *Longevity in Leadership: Essential Qualities of Longtime Leaders*. Abilene Christian University Press, 2016.

Lyon, K. Brynolf. "Faith and Development in Late Adulthood." In *Human Development and Faith: Life-Cycle Stages of Body, Mind, and Soul*, edited by Felicity B. Kelcourse. Chalice Press, 2004.

Mark, Olwyn. *Passing On Faith*. Theos, 2016.

McCall, Larry E. *Grandparenting with Grace: Living the Gospel with the Next Generation*. New Growth Press, 2019.

Meyers, Patty. *Live, Learn, Pass It On! The Practical Benefits of Generations Growing Together in Faith*. Discipleship Resources, 2006.

Miller-Day, Michelle. *Communication among Grandmothers, Mothers, and Adult Daughters: A Qualitative Study of Maternal Relationships*. Lawrence Erlbaum Associates Publishers, 2004.

Minkin, Rachel, Kim Parker, Juliana Menasce Horowitz, and Carolina Aragao, *Parents' Relationship with Their Young Adult Children*. Pew Research Center, 2023.

Parks, Sharon. *The Critical Years: The Young Adult Search for a Faith to Live By*. Harpers & Row Publishers, 1986.

Peterson, Eugene. *The Message*. NavPress, 2002.

Phillips, Godfrey E. *The Transmission of the Faith*. Lutterworth Press, 1946.

Pocta, David. *Cries from the Wilderness: Reimagining Church Culture in an Age of Uncertainty*. Lexington Books, 2024.

Rice, Wayne. *Long-Distance Grandparenting: Nurturing the Faith of Your Grandchildren When You Can't Be There in Person*. Bethany House Publishers, 2019.

Shaughnessy, Michael. *The Strategic Grandparent: Making a Difference*. The Word Among Us Press, 2020.

Shirley, Chris. *Family Ministry and the Church: A Leader's Guide for Ministry through Families*. Randall House, 2018.

Smith, Christian, and Amy Adamczyk. *Handing Down the Faith: How Parents Pass Their Religion On to the Next Generation*. Oxford University Press, 2021.

Smith, Christian, and Melina L. Denton. *Soul Searching: The Religious and Spiritual Lives of American Teenagers*. Oxford University Press, 2005.

Smith, Christian, Bridget Ritz, and Michael Rotolo. *Religious Parenting: Transmitting Faith and Values in Contemporary America*. Princeton University Press, 2020.

Smith, Steven R. "Growing Old in an Age of Transition." In *Old Age in Preindustrial Society*, edited by Peter N. Stearns. Holmes & Meier Publishers, 1982.

Strauss, William, and Neil How. *Generations: The History of America's Future, 1584–2069*. Quill William Morrow, 1991.

Strommen, Merton P., and Richard A. Hardel. *Passing On the Faith: A Radical New Model for Youth and Family Ministry*. Saint Mary's Press, 2000.

Thurman, Chris. *Pop's Advice: Godly Guidance for My Grandkids . . . and Everyone Else*. WestBow Press, 2022.

Tinsley, Barbara R., and Ross D. Parke. "Grandparents as Support and Socialization Agents." In *Beyond the Dyad*, edited by Michael Lewis. Plenum Press, 1984.

Troll, Lillian E. "Grandparents: The Family Watchdogs." In *Family Relationships in Later Life,* edited by Timothy H. Brubaker. Sage Publishing, 1983.

Troll, Lillian E., Sheila J. Miller and Robert C. Atchley. *Families in Later Life*. Wadsworth Publishing Company, 1979.

Vermulst, A. A., A. J. L. L. de Brock, and R. A. H. van Zutphen. "Transmission of Parenting across Generations." In *The Psychology of Grandparenthood: An International Perspective*. Routledge, 1991.

Westerhoff, John H., III. *Will Our Children Have Faith?* Morehouse Publishing, 2000.

Wilcox, W. Bradford. *Soft Patriarchs, New Men: How Christianity Shapes Fathers and Husbands.* University of Chicago Press, 2004.

Willigen, John van, and Narender K. Chadha. *Social Aging in a Delhi Neighborhood*. Bergin & Garvey, 1999.

Witkin, Georgia. *The Modern Grandparent's Handbook: The Ultimate Guide to the New Rules of Grandparenting*. New American Library, 2012.